ULTIMATE BASS FISHING LIBRARY

SEASONAL PATTERNS FOR CATCHING BASS

A YEAR-ROUND GUIDE TO LOCATING
AMERICA'S NO. 1 GAMEFISH

LAKE BUENA VISTA, FLORIDA

INTRODUCTION

HAVE YOU EVER SUFFERED MENTAL GRIDLOCK IN THE midst of what should be the picture perfect springtime day for catching a trophy largemouth? And what about the countless times when the weatherman missed the forecast, blowing your game plan just hours before a weekend tournament?

Even the pros have head-scratching moments like the scenarios listed above. But the experts are quick to adapt to most any situation. After all, they spend hundreds of hours fishing in extreme weather conditions at BASS tournaments held from California to New York.

Metaphorically, it has been said that Bassmaster tournaments are the collective setting where the expertise and ingenuity of the pros, and all the trials and tribulations they face in competition, are poured into a huge funnel. What drips from the end is pure, undiluted bass fishing knowledge.

And that knowledge is converted into the words that are bound into the pages of this hybrid edition of *Bassmaster*. You will not find a more complete reference guide for solving the perplexing riddles bass fishermen face over the course of the four seasons.

This book goes beyond the basics of seasonal patterns and delves into the challenging scenarios that make you cringe when you see the weather forecast. The pros routinely prevail — regardless of the weather — and so can you by following their advice.

Another imposing question bass anglers face, no matter how familiar they are with a fishery, is "where do I start?" The tips of the pros revealed in the pages that follow will put you on the fast track to ending the hunt for bass so you can begin the catching.

And speaking of catching, the smallmouth bass is arguably the gamest of all the bass. But they have certain quirks that can't be overlooked, especially when compared to the more adaptable largemouth. Rely on this book as your guide to bronzebacks when the going gets tough.

Man-made impoundments are the most popular locales for bass fishing. Natural lakes, aging impoundments, rivers and tidal areas are oftentimes overlooked because they take a back seat in the popularity contest of bass fisheries. Tap into their potential by studying the articles featuring these unique fisheries.

Regardless of where and when you go fishing, this book will help you expand your bass angling horizons. And undoubtedly make you a better fisherman.

Copyright 2003 by BASS

Published in 2003 by BASS
PO BOX 10000
Lake Buena Vista, FL 32830

Editor In Chief:
Dave Precht

Editor:
James Hall

Managing Editor:
Craig Lamb

Editorial Assistant:
Althea Goodyear

Art Director:
Rick Reed

Designers:
Laurie Willis, Leah Cochrane,
Bill Gantt, Nancy Lavender

Illustrators:
Chris Armstrong, Shannon Barnes,
Lenny McPherson

Photography Manager:
Gerald Crawford

Contributing Writers:
Wade Bourne, Mark Hicks,
Bruce Ingram, Michael Jones,
Bob McNally, Steve Price,
Steve Quinlan, Jeff Samsel, Louie Stout,
Tim Tucker, Don Wirth, Jack Wollitz

Contributing Photographers:
Wade Bourne, Soc Clay,
Gerald Crawford, Tom Evans,
James Hall, Mark Hicks, Bruce Ingram,
Michael Jones, Bill Lindner,
Peter Mathiesen, Bob McNally,
Dave Precht, Steve Price, Steve Quinlan,
Jeff Samsel, Louie Stout, Tim Tucker,
Don Wirth, Jack Wollitz

Copy Editors:
Laura Harris, Debbie Salter

Manufacturing Manager:
Bill Holmes

Marketing:
Betsy B. Peters

**Vice President &
General Manager, BASS:**
Dean Kessel

Printed on American paper by
R.R. Donnelley & Sons Co.

ISBN 1-890280-02-X

WEATHER PATTERNS, structure and cover, fishery makeup and bass behavior all lend pieces to the puzzle of catching bass. Read on for help in solving these riddles.

CONTENTS

FINDING BASS

End the search for bass
by knowing when to look where ...

FISH A FAMILIAR AREA as a confidence builder before moving up to more advanced tactics.

ADVANCED BASS HUNTING

Raise the bar on your fishing skills with these tips from the pros

AT FIRST GLANCE, the lake seems filled with all manner of fishy-looking places: brushy points, rocky shorelines, protected coves, even scattered grass. Mark Davis, however, isn't paying attention to any of this; he's studying the sky, watching for clouds.

The points and coves aren't really interesting to Ken Cook, either, at least not just now. He's looking at the water itself, searching for something with a little more green in it.

Larry Nixon's eyes are "glued" to the depthfinder as he passes the points and rocky shoreline. He wants to find a creek channel. Robert Hamilton is looking at his water temperature gauge. And Alton Jones is studying a map.

What is this? Why aren't these top BASS pros stopping to fish the coves, the points or the rocky shorelines?

The answer is that many of them actually have a favorite type of cover or structure, or a water or weather condition that takes precedence over anything else they may find. When they launch for the first time on a lake that's new to them, or even where they haven't fished recently, this is how they spend the first few hours.

ROBERT HAMILTON: TEMPERATURE

The 1992 Bassmaster Classic champion is a temperature watcher, especially in spring and fall. Because water temperature strongly influences the metabolism of bass, and because water temperature can vary considerably from one spot to another on the same lake, Hamilton uses

ADVANCED BASS tactics begin with finding repetition in a basic strategy — like keying on isolated brushpiles when main lake pockets are the fundamental pattern.

Speed Reeling Points

■ **Type of lake** — Large impoundment in the East.

■ **Features** — Expansive areas of both deep and shallow cover, including stumps, brush and rocks.

■ **Time of year** — Midsummer.

■ **Best pattern** — Use electronics to scan long tapering points on the main lake and in major creeks for stumps or rocks on the bottom. Catch bass by speed-reeling deep diving crankbaits over the cover. Hold the boat over 30 to 35 feet of water and cast up the point, into 6 to 8 feet. Bass will rise up to take the bait, and strikes are jarring. If crankbaits don't work, comb the same spots with Carolina rigged lizards or grubs.

■ **Key to success** — Concentrate on points that face upstream. These are primary feeding areas for bass, since current pushes baitfish onto the structure.

his temp gauge to choose his fishing areas.

"In spring, I look for warmer water, because the bass are moving shallow," he explains, "while in fall I look for cooler water. A variation of just 2 or 3 degrees can make a major difference in how bass act, so I spend a lot of time checking several creeks and bays. Dingy water absorbs heat faster, so I also look for this condition in spring; in fall, I want clear water."

Hamilton's preferred fishing temperature range for either season is from 55 to about 70 degrees, which is when the bass are most active.

RANDY DEARMAN: LAKE LEVELS

This veteran Texas pro always pays close attention to a lake's water level. If the lake is rising, he knows bass will also rise. If the level is falling, however, bass will move out to the first cover or structure available.

"Studying the water level does not tell me which lures to use or even a specific place to fish," says Dearman. "What it does tell me is how the bass will be acting and the types of water they will move to.

"The faster the water level changes, the faster the bass react," adds the guide on Lake Livingston, Texas. "I remember a BASS event held on Sardis Reservoir where the water was rising 12 inches per day. Overnight, the bass moved nearly a half mile

from one shoreline to the 'new' shoreline."

Large and small bass both will move, notes Dearman, although big bass seem to move faster during falling water. The movement is lakewide, and need not be very great to cause bass to change locations.

Dearman always picks a particular landmark on the bank near the launching ramp and checks the water level against it each morning. If he can't find anything to mark the level, he drives a stick into the beach at the waterline.

KEN COOK: WATER COLOR

A former fisheries biologist and the winner of the 1991 Bassmaster Classic, Cook looks at the water itself, searching for plankton. Because plankton represents the base of the food chain, a high concentration of plankton means a higher population of bait — and gamefish.

"Actually, I look for the transition zone between clear and muddy water, which generally represents the optimum growing conditions for plankton," explains the Oklahoma pro.

"I look for greenish water where I can see my white spinnerbait from about 3 to 6 feet deep. If the spinnerbait disappears from view in a foot of water, it's too muddy, and if I can still see it deeper than 6 feet, it's too clear. I look somewhere else."

Cook adds that studying water clarity is especially important during summer when plankton grows quickly. He usually progresses toward the upper end of a lake, then into a tributary creek, until he finds the conditions he desires.

"In the winter months, plankton does not grow as quickly, but it is still worth looking for," he explains. "On many lakes, some tributaries will be much more fertile than others. On Lake Livingston, which overall is a muddy lake, the top three finishers fished the same creek during a BASS invitational event, and if you ever fish Lake Mead in Nevada, you know that one of the best areas is Vegas Wash, because it isn't as clear as the rest of the lake."

MARK DAVIS: WEATHER PATTERNS

The 1995 Bassmaster Classic champion and Angler of the Year, Mark Davis pays a lot of attention to the sky while he's fishing — he knows that past and present weather conditions will tell him how bass are acting.

"Bass react very quickly to weather changes, even something like cloud changes," he explains. "For instance, if it's been cloudy for several days and suddenly becomes clear, bass will move to cover or deeper water within a few hours, so I know I'll have to change lures or techniques.

"If it has been clear and then becomes cloudy, bass disperse from cover almost immediately and become more active. If they're along the shoreline, many will begin roaming up and down that shore, so it's a good time to use topwater lures."

Bass normally react two ways to spring and summer thunderstorms, continues Davis. "Normally, just before a big storm hits, big bass become active," he explains, "but if there is prolonged thunder and lightning as storms roll around a lake, the bass become very inactive."

Davis even looks at the clouds when he's fishing at night. "Bass don't bite well on bright moonlit nights," he says, "but if the moon happens to go behind the clouds, they'll become active — just as

they do when clouds cover the sun during the day. You'll even find bass more active on a bright night if you fish banks shaded from the moonlight."

ALTON JONES: TRIBUTARIES

A former guide on Richland Chambers Reservoir in north-central Texas and a top contender on the Bassmaster Tournament Trail, Jones looks for tributary creeks when he's on any lake. Many other pros do the same thing, but Jones has specific requirements for his creeks.

"I look for creeks with a channel at least 8 feet deep and at least a mile long," he says. "The creek has to have limited runoff, which means the water level and water quality will remain fairly stable, and I want a creek that has good wood, grass or rock cover.

"If I can find such a creek, I know it will have a resident population of bass all year."

When he fishes these types of creeks, Jones begins at the mouth and fishes to the back, going all the way in on one side and back out on the opposite side. His primary lure choices are spinnerbaits, shallow crankbaits and jigs.

"Most of the creeks I fish tend to be from mid-lake to the upper end, simply because most lower-lake creeks are shorter," he continues. "The real

MARK DAVIS moves to deeper water if the weather turns clear after a period of cloudy weather.

Preseason Scouting

For decades, anglers have used two tools in their search for productive fishing spots — a topographic map and a depthfinder. By studying a topo map, an angler can identify potential bass-holding structures. Then he can pinpoint their exact locations with a depthfinder. Often, it is a long, tedious process, but obviously a necessary one.

There is, however, another way to locate quality structure and cover in a great many of the lakes across America. It is often called "preseason scouting," and it involves little more than visually studying the features of a lake during periods of drawdown or drought, when the water level is low.

Pat Bankston of Sugar Hill, Ga., has been studying bass-holding structure for more than two decades. He has, in fact, utilized that knowledge to catch more than 200 spotted bass in excess of 4 pounds, and he currently holds the Georgia record for spotted bass with an 8-pound, 1/2-ounce spot he caught in 1985 from the deep water structures of Lake Lanier.

Bankston's low water scouting technique is a planned, methodical approach that not only helps him identify potential bass cover, but also helps him locate it again once the lake is at normal pool.

To organize his data so that he will be able to locate structure after the lake level is raised, Bankston creates a notebook with details of each lake he fishes. The notebooks contain hand-drawn maps of structure, photographs to aid in locating structure once submerged, and a plethora of notes.

On his scouting forays, Bankston carries a topographical map and a notebook to draw inset maps to illustrate isolated cover, like brushpiles. He also carries a camera for taking snapshots of exposed structure.

PRESEASON SCOUTING for bass begins in midwinter when exposed shorelines reveal hidden jewels like isolated wood.

Before Bankston begins his scouting trip, he divides the lake into logically defined sections and then plans his trip so that he can scout each section in order. Each segment of this notebook features one section of the lake.

As an example, let's say that Bankston is scouting a small creek arm off the main lake. He will first draw a rough map of the entire area, and then begin filling in pertinent data. He will map the course of the creek channel, noting bends and any natural cover that might be associated with the channel. Next, he visually locates any key structure he believes will hold fish and illustrates accordingly on his map.

Onshore landmarks are included to help him "triangulate" locations so he can find the structures once the water level is raised. Finally, photographs are taken of the entire section and then of each structure Bankston deems important. When taking photographs, it is important to include sufficient onshore images so that the photos are meaningful when viewed at a later date.

The hand-drawn map is then placed in a vinyl page protector, and the accompanying photographs are slipped into the protector as well. In this fashion, all of the data Bankston has collected for this one particular section of the lake is kept together, organized, visible and easily accessible. A three ring binder holds these pages of material in a logical, meaningful order.

Anglers new to this form of scouting would be well advised to first take a look at those areas that have consistently produced fish for them in the past. By studying these areas during the drawdown, you can easily perceive the types of structures that tend to hold bass on your lake. The final step, then, is to look for similar structure around the lake.

key areas in any of the creeks are the insides and outsides of the channel bends, and heavy cover. When the bass are shallow, they're relating to the cover, and I can catch them with a spinnerbait or a jig. But if they're deep and relating to structure, I use the crankbait.

"I'm not fishing for really large bass, but instead, I'm looking for schools of resident fish."

DAVID WHARTON: VEGETATION

Wharton, a former guide on Sam Rayburn Lake and winner of several BASS events, has made a living fishing grass for nearly three decades. Naturally, he looks for vegetation wherever he fishes.

"Vegetation provides food and cover for baitfish as well as bass, and it helps concentrate the fish," he explains. "If you locate grass along the shoreline, on the surface or even under the surface, you're close to bass."

Wharton generally concentrates on the edges of grasslines — the inside edge in spring and the outside edge in summer — where he fishes spinnerbaits or jigs. With edges often extending hundreds of yards across a lake, it's critical to note the conditions whenever the first fish is caught.

"Bass are attracted to points, cuts and other changes along a grassline," Wharton explains, "but just as often, the change may be more subtle, such

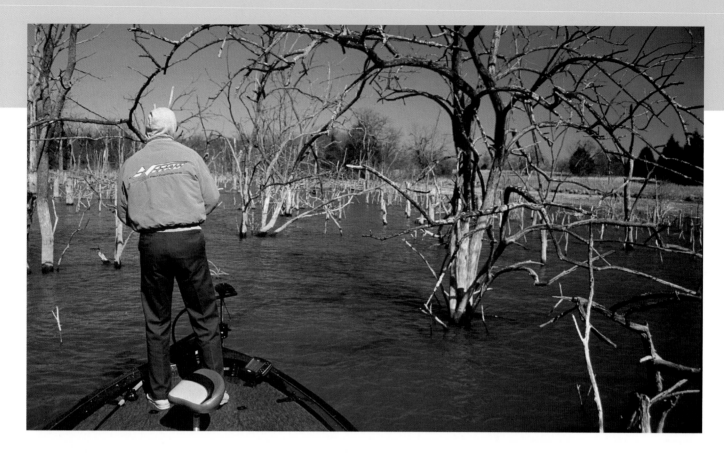

as a slight difference in the depth, an angle where the wind hits the grass differently, or perhaps where a creek comes by. Don't look just at the grass itself, but at everything around you."

At other times the key may be lure presentation. Wharton changes spinnerbait weights and blade combinations as well as his retrieve speeds until something clicks.

LARRY NIXON: DROPOFFS

Nixon, winner of more than $1 million in BASS earnings and champion of the 1983 Bassmaster Classic, likes plastic worm fishing as well as anything, so he looks for places to use those lures, primarily along creek channels and ditches.

"What I'm keying on is the preference bass have for shallow water and deep water close together," he explains. "I'm not specifically fishing the edge of the channel itself, but close to it.

"If you don't have any idea where to start looking for bass on a lake, locate a potential spawning area and then gradually move out toward deeper water until you find a good ditch or channel drop. When you find this, you're close to bass, no matter what season of the year you're fishing."

To better organize his search pattern, Nixon's

summer fishing is generally from the channel to the far shore, an area he terms the "shallow side" of a lake because it is often more like a broad flat. He looks for underwater structure and cover like humps, rocks and brushpiles he can fish not only with a plastic worm but also with a crankbait or spinnerbait.

In winter, he fishes the opposite side of the channel — the side closest to the shore — which he calls the "deep side" of a lake. Again, he is keying on a depth change, but this time it's a more abrupt change.

"Generally, this water is slightly deeper, and in the fall and winter this side is usually more reliable, because it tends to have more vertical banks the bass prefer this time of year," he explains. "This holds true whether you're fishing the main lake channel or one of the tributaries."

WHAT TO LOOK FOR

Obviously, these pros look for other key elements that may help them establish where bass are hiding and what they'll hit.

In your own fish finding explorations, you would do well to keep a sharp eye out for these clues to bass locations. Then you'll be hunting for bass the way the pros do.

FINDING A proverbial needle in a haystack — like a channel winding through dense timber — is key to success in advanced bass hunting.

USE A noisemaker, such as a buzzbait, to make the bass come to you.

SEARCH BAIT SAVVY
Use these tactics to end your search for bass

WHEN SEARCHING FOR BASS, most anglers move from spot to spot, trying different lures, retrieves and presentations as they go. On a good day, they'll eventually find something that works.

But expert bass fishermen, people whose livelihoods depend on finding bass fast, know that certain lures greatly improve their chances of locating groups of aggressive bass. These "search baits" may not be the lures the fishermen will rely on to fill a limit. Instead, the baits are primarily used to cause fish to give away their locations.

"When you fish a search bait correctly around a bunch of fish," notes 1991 Bassmaster Classic winner Ken Cook, "it's going to draw a reaction from one of them. I may not catch that fish, but the reaction it draws lets you know there are bass nearby. Knowing that, I will often change my presentation in order to fish that area more thoroughly."

Like Cook, Larry Nixon believes the key to

finding fish is selecting the proper search bait for the job. Using that tool correctly and asking the right questions, the seasoned tournament pro finds fish quicker than the inexperienced angler who is haphazardly running a bank.

PICKING THE RIGHT TOOL

Nixon takes a systematic approach when selecting a search bait. The former Classic winner first considers the predominant seasonal pattern. "Having considered the season," he adds, "I have an idea of where the bass should be. I then choose the lure that covers the water most efficiently."

Which conditions does Nixon deem important? Foremost, he considers water clarity.

"If the water is colored you're going to be searching for fish in relatively shallow water. On the other hand, in extremely clear water, the fish will most likely be deeper."

Most bass anglers are able to fish a search bait with reasonable effectiveness when bass are shallow. However, on many reservoirs, bass hold in deeper water during the heat of the summer.

"This is when you have to slow down your search and fish more deliberately," explains Nixon. "It's a bit harder to place and keep a search bait in that deeper strike zone."

Nixon's second consideration is the size of the bass' strike zone.

He says it's necessary to determine quickly whether the bass are in the mood to chase a bait, and how far they're willing to move to get it. In fall and spring he believes spinnerbaits, topwaters and lipless crankbaits are excellent search baits. In winter, when bass are typically less active, bottom-bumping, suspending and falling lures that stay in the strike zone longer are better.

Because of its effectiveness in both shallow and relatively deep water, Nixon finds the spinnerbait to be one of the most versatile search baits. "If conditions are right," he adds, "the spinnerbait can be used as a search bait year-round. You can do so many different things with that bait and still match the depth of water you're targeting."

DEEP OR SHALLOW

Cook believes the function of the search bait goes beyond simply catching fish. "You're looking for water that holds bass," says Cook. You're looking for the *right* water, including the right depth changes and types of cover."

The search bait becomes especially important when probing deep structure. When fishing relatively deep water in summer, Cook usually looks for a single key spot — such as a stump or rock — that will concentrate the fish. Many anglers, after locating a good dropoff, stop the search there, mistakenly assuming they will catch a bunch of fish from it.

According to the Oklahoma pro, fishing a deep water edge is similar to fishing a shallow bank. You wouldn't expect to catch fish all along that bank — instead, you look for a key feature along the bank that concentrates the fish.

Right Choice, Wrong Bait

A number of baits can be used as search baits. Often, choosing the right one is only the first step. Ken Cook explains, "My favorite search bait is the spinnerbait, because it can be fished shallow as well as deep. Still, you have to match the spinnerbait to the water you're fishing."

Within a group of baits — like spinnerbaits and crankbaits — there are a variety of options from which an angler can choose. When choosing a crankbait, it's necessary to match the running depth and buoyancy of the model with the situation you're fishing. Similarly, when choosing a spinnerbait, the combination of blades and head weight must match the application.

"If I'm fishing relatively shallow water in Lake Okeechobee and I know the fish aren't going to hit a really fast bait," explains Cook, "I go to a bait I can fish slowly. For that job, I will fish a 1/4-ounce bait with relatively large blades. On the other hand, if I'm fishing deep ledges on Kentucky Lake, I like a bait that will get down to the targeted depth and cover the water quickly — a 1-ounce spinnerbait with small blades."

Hunting For Schools

■ **Type of lake** — Lowland reservoir in the East.
■ **Features** — Average depth is less than 10 feet; grassbeds and cypress stumps are the two main types of cover.
■ **Time of year** — Fall.
■ **Best pattern** — Bass location depends on the water level. In high water, hunt for bass around shallow cover with spinnerbaits, shad pattern crankbaits and other search lures. If the water is low, head to the upper end and flip 3/4-ounce black/blue jig-and-pigs around cypress trees and laydowns.
■ **Key to success** —Cover water and hit plenty of targets. Keep moving to find areas where bass are concentrated. Watch for surface schooling activity in main lake areas, and cast to feeding bass with topwaters.

BASS MOVE TO isolated cover to ambush their prey at feeding time.

FAST-FOOD STOPS FOR BASS

Make the most of prime feeding areas with these tips

RANDY HOWELL CALLS THEM the "temporary rest stops" of the fishing world. Bud Pruitt admits that he doesn't understand why bass move to and away from them.

Both hotshot BASS pros are discussing bass feeding grounds, and despite the ambivalence these anglers express about these locales, they agree that feeding grounds are worth learning more about.

When Pruitt once won a major title at Alabama's Lake Wheeler, he did so by targeting a pair of what he termed "man-made feeding grounds."

Just how does he define these types of areas and, more importantly, how does he go about fishing them?

BUD PRUITT searches out man-made ambush points when the real thing is unavailable.

Textbook Feeding Areas

■ **Type of lake** — Large natural lake in Florida.

■ **Features** — Abundant emergent weeds in shallower areas and hydrilla beds in deeper water.

■ **Time of year** — May.

■ **Best pattern** — After spawning, bass group in schools around open water hydrilla to feed on shad. Look for grass edges, boat lanes or openings in hydrilla beds. Also, be alert for any place (canal mouths, neckdowns, etc.) that has current or prevailing winds; these will concentrate shad. Watch for feeding activity, such as baitfish flipping or bass splashing.

■ **Key to success** — Bass will be in textbook feeding areas, and they'll be there in groups. When you catch one bass, others are likely to be in the same spot.

MAN-MADE FEEDING GROUNDS

"I define man-made feeding grounds as places that are basically pancake-flat and would be totally barren of good-size bass unless cover is placed there," Pruitt says. "Crawfish, bluegill and small bass may come to live there, but generally bass over 2 pounds do not, until objects such as concrete, tires, brush, or Christmas trees are planted on the bottom.

"For some reason, and I can't explain why, something will trigger the bass to come to these areas and feed. Sometimes it may be the appearance of shad or perhaps it is the moon phase. Some man-made areas never have bass show up, no matter how much cover is added. And I know of one place where a guy merely dumped a 2-by-4 on the center of a flat and the bass flock there now."

Pruitt believes his Lake Wheeler experience was typical of how bass move in and out from man-made

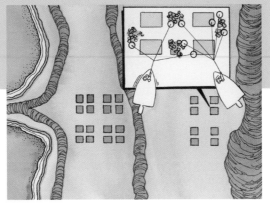

BUD PRUITT'S main feeding ground on Lake Wheeler, at the base of pilings on a shallow flat, attracted both smallmouth and largemouth.

feeding grounds. The first day he worked one area, the fish did not show until 9 a.m. Throughout the rest of the day, however, the bass moved up and departed in regular waves.

The Texas pro's man-made feeding ground had some distinct characteristics: A steel transmission-line tower rose over a jumble of concrete slabs. About 150 yards to one side was the main channel; a creek channel meandered some 300 to 400 yards away on the other side. Stumps dotted the general area, but were scarce in the vicinity of the tower.

Interestingly, both smallmouth and largemouth gravitated toward the concrete slabs — an indicator, notes Pruitt, that both types of black bass utilize feeding grounds. The smallies held behind rocks close to a depth change, while the largemouth grouped on the shallow end of the cover.

Pruitt follows an unusual seasonal approach when fishing the feeding flats. He doesn't try to determine whether the fish are in a prespawn, spawn or postspawn mode.

Sometimes arrival of bass is based on the advent of shad. Thus, Pruitt ties on a medium running crankbait, a 3/4-ounce Rat-L-Trap or a spinnerbait. All three types worked well for him in the Alabama tournament and have elsewhere. Pruitt prefers a moderate to slow retrieve as these artificials bump into the cover.

Come summer, bass found on man-made feed-

ing grounds become more predictable in their movements.

"I only fish for these bass early and late in the day in warm water," he says. "They move in early and leave quickly. They typically don't come back until the evening. The rest of the day, expect to catch bass only occasionally — really, it may not be worth your time even to check out such an area."

Pruitt relies on plastic worms and spinnerbaits to take bass from these dining flats during warm weather. He patiently crawls a worm over the cover or slow rolls a spinnerbait.

In fall, man-made feeding grounds pay off only when the wind blows. Wind-generated currents push baitfish across the cover, and the bass occasionally move up, engulf their prey and return to holding areas. In this situation, Pruitt likes to fish spinnerbaits and small crankbaits.

TEMPORARY REST STOPS

Howell offers an interesting analogy to describe feeding grounds: "My favorite feeding ground is one that is sort of like those rest stops on interstate highways," he says. "Bass travel up a creek channel and normally pull up to a flat several times a day, just like people travel down an interstate and pull over to a rest stop ever so many hours."

Actually, his fishing holes are more like fast-food restaurants for bass. The fish don't stay long in any one spot, but when they visit, they're there to eat. But what triggers feeding periods?

"The appearance of shad is the reason bass move to this kind of feeding ground," explains

BASS MOVE FROM three directions onto Randy Howell's favorite type of feeding ground with the fish following creek channels to reach the common area. (Far right) KEN COOK looks for bass near saddles (A) or depressions in humps that block movement between deep channels and the shallows. Rows of rocks (B) create productive funnels.

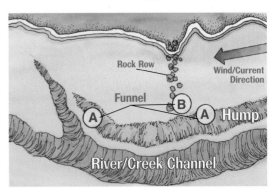

Howell. "In the spring, for example, shad follow the channels or the roadbed up to the flat itself, and the bass follow the food.

"I like to slow roll a 1/2-ounce spinnerbait with a chartreuse-and-white skirt across the flat of a prime feeding ground. Since the shad spread out across such a flat, hits could happen anytime during the retrieve."

Like Bud Pruitt, Howell believes the stage of the spawn is not relevant for flats fishing — only actively feeding fish use a flat. To catch them, an angler only has to be present at the right times. Howell adds that fishermen must have the patience to wait sometimes an hour or more for another group of fish to move in.

With the arrival of summer, he says many people feel that shallow "rest stop" feeding flats become too warm to entice bass. In truth, he claims that plenty of bass journey to these locales during hot weather — but they use them in a way that's different from other times of the year.

"Using my favorite feeding flat scenario as an example, the bass there in hot weather group in three different ways," he says. "One group stays on the bottom of the channels, another group suspends in the channels and a third concentration roams about just under the surface in the channels.

"The schooling fish are the hardest to catch because each individual fish just targets a single baitfish at a time. I recommend that people ignore them. But periodically, the other two groups of bass will move out of the channels to the edges of the feeding flats, and that's when they are vulnerable."

Generally, this movement takes place at daylight and dusk, but it can occur in the middle of the day as well. For low light conditions, Howell prefers a topwater chugger.

To extend the morning bite or to probe the sides of the flat later in the day, Howell relies on a Carolina rig. The Alabama pro crisscrosses the flat with this rig and is especially attuned to any slight changes in the bottom.

During autumn, Howell notes that bass still come to rest-stop flats two or three times daily.

Targeting The Funnels

BRIDGES CREATE a type of compression area that concentrates the bass in one particular area.

Funnels, or compression areas, are places where bass are often most easily located and most vulnerable to being caught. Pros like Ken Cook know that targeting funnels is a shortcut to the most likely bass concentration zones — areas inhabited by bass throughout the year.

"The physical definition of a funnel is some physical obstruction that narrows down a travelway," Cook says. "Because bass are such edge-oriented animals, they will generally associate with the edges, whether it be the bottom or surface of the water, or treelines, grasslines and ditches.

"When I think of funnels, what comes to mind is a convex piece of structure that sticks up off the bottom of the lake and restricts travel through the area between the two major surfaces — the surface of the water and the bottom of the lake. It's an ideal situation for a predator like a bass to find its food and have an advantage.

"Bass, because of their opportunistic nature and the efficiency with which they are a predator, are always willing and able to find a place where they have the advantage."

Cook believes that the smaller size of a funnel makes it easier to pinpoint key hot spots. But a compact area may be too confined to support several fish.

"With a funnel, the compression factor is the deal," Cook says. "But the more factors that come into play to physically restrict travel, the better a funnel will be. That might include several obstructions, like a channel edge, fencerow or ditch coming together in one particular area. But it could also include the thermocline, which restricts bass to a certain level. The more of those things you have to your advantage, the better the funnel is likely to be. And a predator like a bass realizes that, too. The more factors you have, the smaller the funnel becomes — even in a large area."

"The bass are very prey-specific then," he says. "When I catch the first one, I look into its mouth and try to determine what it has been feeding on.

"If it's a crawfish, I use a Carolina rig with a plastic crawfish, obviously. If it is a shad, I tie on a Norman DD22, which really digs into the bottom. A big lipped, deep diving crankbait like this deflects very erratically when retrieved through shallow water. And when I stop the DD22, it floats up very quickly. This bait also offers the advantage of covering large expanses of a rest-stop flat at a time."

IF YOU KNOW BASS are feeding on shad, it's a sure bet that they will hit a shad-colored crankbait of the appropriate size.

BREAKING DOWN BIG WATER

Narrow your options through these approaches

ONE OF THE NEVER-ENDING questions among bass fishermen is how to locate fish on large impoundments. Pose that question to two very successful bass fishermen, and you'll get two conflicting answers:

"My first step is to determine what part of a lake will 'fish to my strengths' — an area that will let me fish the way I want to fish," says Mike McClelland.

"I have never looked specifically for water that I would like to catch fish in. I study the overall lake and take what it has to offer," adds Richard McCarty.

What is most interesting is that McClelland and McCarty eventually end up at the same place — catching bass — even though they take different routes to get there. Anglers should find bits of advice from these opposing viewpoints that can help them locate fish in big water faster.

PLAY TO YOUR STRONG SUIT

"It's important to find water I like to fish because it gives me an immediate sense of confidence," says McClelland. "When you start out with a feeling of confidence, you simply fish better because you're more relaxed.

"I like to fish dingy water, because I believe bass are easier to catch under those conditions. This is especially true on clear water lakes, like Table Rock or Bull Shoals in Arkansas and Missouri. In off-color water, you can use heavier line and pretty much forget about finesse techniques. I like to throw a spinnerbait because I can cover a lot of water quickly with it, and when bass are shallow in dingy water, it's hard to find a better lure than a spinnerbait."

McClelland looks for his dingy water by studying maps to find large tributary creeks. On a clear impoundment, for example, he expects to find dingy water in the headwaters at the upper end of the lake.

"I like to pick one general area of a lake and learn as much as I can about it during the practice days (for a tournament)," he explains. "The area must have at least one major creek, and it must have a number of main lake points and coves. In the spring and fall, creeks will normally be more important than lake points, while in summer and

Three Steps To Finding Bass

Mike McClelland's procedures are easy for any bass fisherman to follow:
1. Pick an area of the lake with a winding tributary and main lake points.
2. Look for dingy water where bass will be shallow.
3. Start with a spinnerbait or crankbait.

winter, the points are more critical because they tend to have deeper water."

Points are key structures for him because bass seem to be especially attracted to them. And they're not very difficult to fish, he adds. He uses a PinPoint trolling motor with built-in sonar that automatically keeps his boat over a certain contour level. "This helps me find and define the points easier than I could by studying them with only a depthfinder," he suggests.

There's more to simply choosing an area that has a big creek, of course. McClelland wants that tributary to have a lot of bends and secondary points, because these tend to concentrate bass. Creeks that run more or less straight mean bass will be scattered, unless there are other features

Up A Winding River

■ **Type of lake** — Deep, clear high-land reservoir.
■ **Features** — Several large, winding tributary arms sport standing timber growing down sloping banks.
■ **Time of year** — Midsummer.
■ **Best pattern** — Concentrate on the main tributaries, looking for gravel bars that roll off into the river channel, normally on the opposite shore from sheer rock bluffs. Use electronics to search for shad schools, and cast to them with deep diving crankbaits. Cast shallow and retrieve deep. Also jig spoons off the bottom or drag spider grubs down the slopes.
■ **Key to success** — Fishing will be twice as good in the tributaries as in the main lake. It's possible for this pattern to produce over 50 bass a day, including some heavyweights.

McCarty's Musts

Richard McCarty looks for three key elements that are conducive for bass to spawn in an area and that hold fish there throughout their lives:
1. A well-defined channel adjacent to a shallow feeding zone.
2. A large area that offers protection from wind.
3. Good water quality.

that concentrate the fish. His map study will also tell him which areas or tributaries have standing timber, although this cover is not always a major consideration for him.

"Certain criteria have different levels of importance at various times of the year," he explains. "For example, I believe baitfish can be very important in locating bass, and you can actually find baitfish by studying a map. In the fall, shad will migrate up the river arms onto the flats and into the backs of pockets and creeks, so you look for features like this when you're trying to isolate a particular section of a lake at that time of year. In other seasons, such as spring, baitfish are not a primary consideration."

When baitfish are a prime consideration, McClelland comes armed with a spinnerbait. "At different times of the year, other lures might be better at locating bass," he continues. "Suspending crankbaits work well in spring, for example. And if I can't find dingy water and have to fish where it's clear, I'll use a Carolina rig with a twin tail Arkie grub."

McClelland's techniques certainly seem easy enough for any bass fisherman to follow. Just pick an area of the lake with a winding tributary and main lake points, look for dingy water where bass will be shallow, and start with a spinnerbait or crankbait.

It's a system a number of pros use successfully along the Bassmaster Tournament Trail.

LOOK FOR SPAWNING GROUNDS

Compare them, however, with the technique practiced by McCarty, a pro and trophy bass guide on Lake Fork, Texas.

"The first thing I do is locate a place where I know bass are going to *start* their life," he emphasizes. "I look at what the lake has to offer and pick one spot that gives fish a lot of options for staying in that area. Most of the time, this will be a tributary creek, but not always. It can also be a large cove or bay, but seldom will it be part of the main lake itself, unless that lake has well-established grassbeds. Vegetation, like hydrilla and milfoil, changes bass habits, because of the excellent habitat it provides."

He looks for several key criteria, elements con-

ON LAKES with standing timber look for open areas where baitfish will school over shallow flats during the fall.

USE BAITFISH IMITATORS like crankbaits in open water, and spinnerbaits in heavy cover for locating bass in the spring and fall.

ducive for bass to spawn in an area and remain there throughout their lives, including a well-defined channel that gives bass a shallow feeding zone with immediate access to deep water; a large area that offers protection from wind; good water quality; and cover.

Of all the ingredients McCarty looks for in a spawning area, the most important is not a hard bottom or even the presence of baitfish (he pays little attention to either when looking for a starting point). Instead, it is water clarity.

"Water clarity determines the depth bass will be using," says McCarty. "Bass want to be able to get below the level of light penetration because, I think, they use the darker water as a type of sanctuary. This is absolutely critical, and I believe this is why shallow water/deep water combinations are good anywhere. Bass use darker water for their own protection.

Another of the criteria McCarty uses to choose a spawning area is cover. The actual spawning area itself does not have to have a lot of cover, but cover of some type must be nearby. It can take the form of stumps, shoreline laydowns, standing timber or brush; he doesn't like to fish boat docks, so he does not include them in his list.

"Cover dictates lure choice," McCarty explains. "I pick a lure that works best in the majority of cover types. If it's rocks or isolated stumps, I'll usually use a crankbait, but if it's vegetation or laydowns, I'll generally use a spinnerbait."

PREPARATION IS THE SECRET

The common element in both approaches is preparation. Both anglers do their homework. McClelland and McCarty each spend hours studying lake maps, and once they're on the water, they spend additional hours just looking at different areas before they ever begin casting.

Every bass angler, regardless of his level of expertise, can do this same type of study, and then choose bits and pieces from both approaches to suit his own style of fishing. As the record proves, each will lead you to bass.

Breaking Down Big Reservoirs

Part of being a professional bass angler is having to fish a variety of waters. Of these, the most complex are man-made reservoirs.

While anglers like 1991 Bassmaster Classic champion Ken Cook use the same methodology in breaking down each type of water, the components of a reservoir system offer more options. From cover and structure to deep and shallow water, the puzzle pieces of man-made impoundments — especially large ones — are simply more numerous.

For Cook, the breakdown process begins before he ever gets to the lake. Based on the time of year and type of lake, he can narrow his search to smaller, more manageable sections of the impoundment. Then, once he gets on the water, Cook can start assessing information that the lake itself provides.

"In summer, you can eliminate a lot of the upper ends of creeks and backs of pockets because the fish can be caught better in the main parts of the lake. In spring, you can ignore much of the main lake areas and focus more on the creeks."

Up to this point, Cook has shrunk the lake horizontally. Now, after choosing a specific section to fish, he must develop some guidelines to compress the lake vertically by determining how deep to fish. This is the next logical progression in finding catchable bass.

The key to the vertical element is nearly always water color. Whether it is muddy, stained or clear or offers a high degree of fertility, sunlight penetration is the engine that operates the whole system. To some extent, bass live in zones of light penetration, observes Cook, with light being the prime ingredient in photosynthesis. It is a process that creates oxygen to support a food chain, which places bass right at the top.

The next component of this bass fishing pattern is the type of cover available. It should be noted, however, that once you determine the most likely fish-holding depth, there are several factors that can affect your estimates.

"Everything interferes with this assumption of depth," warns Cook. "If you change areas of the lake, the light penetration may change. If you have a lot of standing timber or other cover that provides shade, the fish may not be as deep."

Another mitigating factor — and an important one to be sure — are the types of forage available. Generally, it's shad, crawfish and bluegill. But in reservoirs, the predominant forage base is often shad. Therefore, the presence of shad and their location is a powerful key in locating the best places to catch bass in a reservoir.

"When you find the plankton, you'll find the shad — and the bass."

SAVVY ANGLERS choose a spinnerbait as a search tool when trying to eliminate unproductive water. Color selection depends on water quality and the dominate forage base.

AFTER STUDYING a map that leads to a potential hot spot, save its location with a GPS.

MAKE THE MOST OF MAPS

Use lake maps to uncover valuable fishing treasures

LEGENDARY TOURNAMENT ANGLER Bill Dance once described lake maps as being "as useful to the modern bass fisherman as treasure maps were to the pirates of the 18th century."

That statement remains true today, even after an evolutionary period that produced amazing technological gains in equipment and achievements in bass fishing know-how. Just as tournament pioneers like Dance discovered in the early years, today's bass angler wouldn't think of going onto a strange lake without a detailed map.

Of course, a map is meaningless to the angler who doesn't understand how bass relate to structure throughout the seasons. But if you know that bass follow points and dropoffs on natural lakes, and points and creek channels on reservoirs to and from spawning areas, a map is going to be a tremendous asset.

"Experienced bass fishermen know how to find the primary areas of a lake by reading a map," adds veteran pro Woo Daves. "The difference occurs when an angler goes on the water with his map and finds the less obvious structure on a potential hot spot."

Not all maps are created equal, say the pros, and many aren't entirely accurate. That's why they are picky about the maps they use.

"Look on the legend and see when the lake was mapped," offers Kevin VanDam, another veteran BASS pro. "Coast Guard and NOAA (National Oceanic and Atmospheric Administration) charts tend to be more reliable. Some of the larger map companies have updated old maps and made them more trustworthy. But if the map is old,

STUDYING A topographic map can reveal the hidden contour lines below an otherwise barren shoreline.

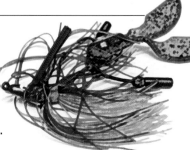

Mapping Out Hot Spots

■ **Type of lake** — Western water storage reservoir.
■ **Features** — Small canyon impoundment known for huge bass.
■ **Time of year** — Fall.
■ **Best pattern** — As fall progresses, bass transition to bank and bottom structure. By midfall, the best spots for big bass are main lake points. Use sonar to scan for cover objects on these points in 12 to 36 feet of water — brush, rocks, stumps, etc. Work these spots with a 3/8-ounce jig-and-pig. Reel the jig slowly across the bottom for best results on bigger fish.
■ **Key to success** — Be meticulous in comparing topo map information with depthfinder readings to find good spots. When checking a spot electronically, note how bass are relating to the structure. Those close to the bottom are catchable.

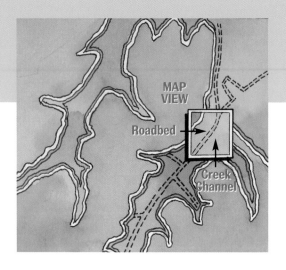

IF YOU CAN find a roadbed leading to a creek channel, chances are that bass will be there.

you'll probably find major discrepancies in what the map shows and what you find out there on the water."

Maps of reservoirs that were built by the U.S. Army Corps of Engineers tend to be even more accurate because they were mapped with more sophisticated techniques. Many man-made lake maps evolved from preimpoundment maps that indicate roadbeds, ponds, buildings, creeks, wooded areas and ditches — features that attract bass.

However, don't expect to find everything in a lake that you see on preimpoundment maps. Engineers often removed trees, demolished roads and bridges or altered the bottom prior to flooding.

Also, older lakes go through many changes over the course of time, some of which are caused by siltation, current, or man-made modifications that occured after the lake was flooded.

FINDING SWEET SPOTS

AFTER THE MAP has led you to the roadbed, use electronics to pinpoint where the fish are relating to this type of cover.

A quality map is a valuable tool for finding areas that will likely hold bass, but it doesn't tell all. Bass pros use maps to identify general areas and types of structure that would likely hold bass during a specific season.

"Knowing the seasonal pattern allows you to eliminate a lot of the lake and concentrate on specific areas," explains VanDam. "Once you've got a general idea of what the fish should be doing, you can study the map for the sections of the lake that should hold the most fish."

In addition, says 10 time Bassmaster

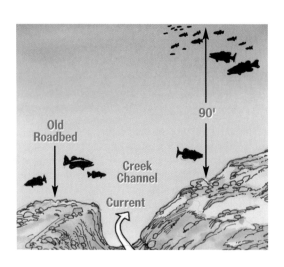

HAVING AN EYE for recognizing symbols like roadbeds and how they relate to breaklines is an important part of map study.

Classic qualifier Guy Eaker, the map allows you to find structure that is conducive to your style of fishing. By targeting "confidence areas," you are less likely to be intimidated by the size of a large body of water.

"I want the confidence area to be a miniature version of the lake itself, offering bass all the same cover and structure options they have in the big water," he describes. "You can fish a confidence area in a few hours and determine one or more patterns. It could take days to do that on the entire lake."

There are other things to consider, says Eaker. If you're fishing shorelines, key on those that have the most irregular features, such as points, coves or indentations. If the lake has a lot of grass, you need to consider secondary features within the grass, such as stumps, channels or points.

Most maps don't show habitat, water quality or other environmental factors that impact a bass' well-being, so you'll need to gather that information beforehand or when you get on the water.

"I need to know the water clarity of a lake to determine the kinds of areas to look for," adds VanDam. "For example, if the water is stained, then I want to concentrate on shallower areas. If it's clear, then I seek the slightly deeper areas."

If he's targeting creeks on a stained section of a lake, for example, VanDam will eliminate the deeper creeks. On the other hand, if the lake is clear, the deeper creeks will support larger numbers of bass, he adds.

Regardless of the season or the water clarity, flats are the focus of VanDam's search. He looks for flats that will provide feeding areas and spawning habitat. Again, water clarity will determine how shallow or deep he begins the search.

"In tournament situations, I need to target areas that will hold enough bass to carry me for a tournament that lasts three or more days," he explains. "So I look for large flats that offer everything the bass prefer that time of year."

With specific areas marked on his map, VanDam will do a quick drive-through of the area, watching for depth changes, visible cover and structure. If it's a large bay or creek, he'll zigzag across offshore structure such as points and dropoffs. If it's a flat with a weedline, a common structure for natural lakes, he'll motor over it while looking for points, turns or changes in depth.

Anglers who rely entirely on the map are making a mistake, he adds. Most anglers can spot the obvious structure, but your depthfinder and eyes will help you find the "sweet spots" that most fishermen overlook. A sweet spot may be a subtle knob sticking off the side of point, a hard bottom or rockpile in a grassline, or a stumprow lining a creek ledge.

VanDam concludes that maps can be more valuable for refining a pattern than they are for locating fishing areas. For example, if he catches fish in pockets along secondary points, he can study the map for more points that have the same characteristics.

"During the spring, pockets along northern banks may be productive because of the warmer water, so I look at the map for more pockets on northern banks," he explains. "Or, if wind is blowing into a spot and is a contributing factor, I can look at how the lake lies and choose structure in other areas where the wind may help my cause."

Find Bass with a Camera

Your home camcorder or digital camera can do more than record memories of special occasions, like Christmas and your kid's birthday parties. These handy electronic aids have a fishing application when used during the wintertime on reservoirs that undergo an annual draw-down during the chilly season.

Recording exposed shorelines has even greater benefit for smallmouth aficionados. Smallmouth bass spend perhaps 90 percent of their lives in 10 feet of water or more, if they can get to it. Even when they're shallow, smallmouth want quick, easy access to deep water. What is more, they like homes with a bottom of hard mud and gravel.

Potential spots can be taped or photographed with references made on lake maps. Following are tips that can be useful when trekking about the shoreline to record future hot spots with a camera.

■ DETERMINE THE LAKE ELEVATION — Lakes are measured in distance above sea level. If the stump you are recording is at the winter pool level of 475 feet, you will know that when the water returns to summer pool of 490 feet, it will be 15 feet deep.

■ DON'T VIDEO A SPOT YOU KNOW BASS WON'T USE — This sounds obvious, but in your rush to video every piece of cover, you may overlook key factors. For example, if you're fishing for smallmouth, concentrate only on those places that provide quick access to deep water.

■ IDENTIFY THE SPOT ON CAMERA — A dry-marker note board can be invaluable in recording the location, name and other information about an area you are filming. Have a buddy stand in front of the camera holding the card, or prop it against a rock.

■ USE A TRIPOD — Let the camera run for several minutes so you can get a good look at each spot. Otherwise, when viewing the video, you'll be constantly rewinding the tape to study the structure.

■ ANALYZE THE SPOT — As you line up the shot, think about where the bass will most likely live on a structure feature. For example, a brushpile on a long, soft-mud flat will not be as good as a brushpile placed close to deep water on a bottom of hard mud and gravel.

WHEN YOU FIND a productive area on the lake you are fishing, notate the spot, the time of year and what you used on your map for future reference.

WHILE OTHER anglers take the easy way out and beat the shallows, go the opposite direction and use an LCD electronic graph as a shortcut to finding bass in deep water.

THE SONAR THREE STEP
It's easier than programming your VCR

I F YOU HAD TO CHOOSE one thing that separates average bass fishermen from great ones it would be the ability to find fish — quickly.

For some veterans, processing information and formulating a game plan are accomplished at a nearly subconscious, intuitive level. However, less-experienced anglers and those who find themselves in difficult situations have to take a slower, step-by-step approach.

This is especially true when dealing with the complexities of sonar operation.

While speed in locating bass may seem like a tournament fishing imperative, it really affects recreational fishermen just as dramatically. Like it or not, the weekend angler functions on a rather tight schedule and probably needs to find his quarry faster than does a competitive fisherman — someone who normally has the benefit of a practice period prior to an event.

But, how do you do it? The first thing to remember is this: Start with the big picture and gradually refine things down to more precise elements. It's like the old riddle about how to eat an elephant: One bite at a time.

In the following three-tier program, the object is to guide an angler from general observations to specific ones in a quick and understandable way. What's more, any bass fisherman, regardless of his or her skill level, can use this program.

The only variable in using this sonar "three-step" is where an angler chooses to begin. For instance, a more experienced fisherman who recognizes the prevailing seasonal pattern can leap frog ahead of a beginning angler who needs more time in eliminating water. But there are times when the more skilled fisherman will need to take a few steps backward if he is to make sense of a confusing situation.

LEVEL 1

For anyone just getting acquainted with their electronics, the search for bass must be narrowed down to the absolute basics: **Find activity at *any* depth.**

Although sonar units will not always show an abundance of gamefish in a productive area, it will almost always tell you if the water being surveyed offers a fertile environment. This is pure, big picture stuff.

However, instead of simply looking for fish activity, the key is to find a complete array of aquatic life from the top of the food chain to the bottom. If your sonar screen does not show any "surface clutter" indicating algae/plankton or baitfish underneath, move on.

The toughest part to this very basic survey is not seeing the proverbial forest for the trees. At this point, you don't need to sweat the details. In fact, it's wise to pull your eyes away from the sonar long enough to see if a particular area is supporting other types of animal activity.

ANALYZING THE LAKE

Of course, getting started is perhaps the most vexing dilemma. Even so, it can be handled rather easily by first breaking the lake down into major habitat areas and then looking for activity in those zones.

Somewhere amongst the available smorgasbord of cover and structure, an activity zone will appear on your sonar screen. But in this search, you're not looking for fish arches at a specific depth or in a certain location. And, you're not looking for something subtle. Instead, the idea is simply to find general, overall activity. Once you're in the right ballpark, then you can expand your search to locate fish concentrations.

After one activity area has been located and fished successfully, the next step is to check out other areas of the lake that offer similar structure and cover. By doing so, you'll be able to see if the activity and bass are dependent on certain conditions being present. This is the very bedrock of pattern fishing.

Seeing Trees On Sonar

■ **Type of lake** — Large, mainstream reservoir in the South.
■ **Features** — Classic structure lake with extensive flats divided by stump-lined creek and river channels.
■ **Time of year** — Midsummer.
■ **Best pattern** — This is prime structure fishing time. Use a depthfinder and a map to locate underwater points where creeks empty into the main river channel. Then look for submerged timber both on these points and downstream along the main channel ledges. The key depth is 12 to 25 feet on the shallow side of these ledges. Work them with deep crankbaits or slow rolled heavy spinnerbaits.
■ **Key to success** — Keep riding over the river ledge and looking for areas that have standing trees. These areas will produce the biggest bass.

USE ELECTRONICS as your underwater eyes for finding the depth range where baitfish are active.

LEVEL 2

At the intermediate level, a fisherman needs to focus on a specific depth range by applying the knowledge acquired through sonar. To find a more precise depth range that offers the greatest amount of gamefish activity, simply turn on your sonar as you slowly motor away from the launch ramp first thing in the morning.

Even if the activity zone occurs at 15 feet over water that is much deeper, the primary activity zone found near the marina will closely approximate this depth throughout the lake. Now, the object is to focus your angling attentions around key structure and cover in this depth range.

If the activity zone is spread over a broader depth range, then a fisherman should concentrate on the depth that best suits his fishing style. It's a case of maximizing your strengths and, in fishing terms, throwing what you know.

Obviously, you can't be too stubborn in resisting a particular depth range or type of lure. Although professional anglers have proved that fish can be taken from nearly any depth, most fishermen need to stack the odds in their favor. To do this effectively, there is no substitute for versatility — selecting the right lure and fishing it at the most productive depth.

LEVEL 3

As described in Levels 1 and 2, the sonar search area is gradually being narrowed as one's skill improves. Levels 1 and 2 ask the fisherman to "focus" on a specific depth range within a general activity zone. In Level 3, the refinement process continues. Now, it becomes a matter of pinpointing a specific part of the structure at a chosen depth range that offers the greatest probability of holding fish.

The ability to quickly find these areas of

USE SONAR in western impoundments for locating offshore arroyos, where fish hold during the summertime.

The Sonar Three Step

Step 1
■ Break the lake down into general areas.
■ Find activity at any depth that shows a full spectrum of life, from bait- to gamefish.
■ Check similar and dissimilar areas to confirm what you have found.

Step 2
■ Focus on the specific depth level where activity is present.
■ Throw what you know.
■ Don't try to make something out of nothing. Fish prime areas with a suitable lure at the proper depth.
■ Sonar also tells you where there is no activity. Use this knowledge to your best advantage.

Step 3
■ Resist the temptation to graph every inch of a fishing location.
■ Find the best area within an area that offers the greatest potential for success.
■ When fish are caught, expand your search area. If not, move on to the next general area, find the key spot there and repeat the process.

"greatest probability" is often what separates those who catch fish from those who do not. In particular, this ability makes an even bigger difference when it comes to unfamiliar waters or during periods of adverse weather conditions. Those anglers who have learned how to pinpoint these smaller, high productive areas — and do it quickly — simply spend more time making high percentage casts.

By the time an angler has reached this level, the specifics shown on sonar are reinforced by where fish are being caught. Now, it becomes a matter of recognizing precisely what features make a difference. For instance, if

bass are being taken from the steep, windy side of main lake points in 12 feet of water — especially those with isolated cover — does it make a lot of sense to fish the entire point? Especially when you're trying to pinpoint the bite?

Clearly, the answer to both questions is "no." If there are no fish on the best area of the structure, why waste time with the rest of it? If there are no catchable bass on a prime contact point, most likely the group of fish using this structure are either not feeding or not in the ideal position. Often it becomes a matter of timing, requiring an angler to keep checking back to determine if and when bass are using a particular spot.

In many ways, the tactics described in Level 3 are comparable to those methods used when fishing visible targets. Specifically, when a skilled fisherman casts first to the most likely fish-holding section of a laydown log, dock or brushpile. If this well-placed offering doesn't garner a response and an angler is trying to maximize his or her fishing time, there is little to be gained from long-shot presentations. However, should a key portion turn up a fish, then a more detailed search is in order.

By pinpointing the key area within an area and by having the confidence to believe in one's fishing abilities, an angler can evaluate a larger piece of structure by what happens in a small section.

WHEN GOING AFTER deep bass with Texas rigged soft plastics, add a bead or clacker weight to the setup. The extra commotion will help bass find your bait if you are slightly off target.

FISHING CONDITIONS

Change is the only constant
in bass fishing ...

CHANGING CONDITIONS AND BASS

When the bass' environment changes, the angler has to adapt as well

LET'S DISCUSS THE METAPHYSICS of bass fishing. Perhaps the only constant in this sport is change. More to the point, *conditions* change. Hour to hour, day to day, week to week, season to season, fishing conditions are in a continual state of upheaval. Frontal passages change water temperature, cloud cover and barometric pressure. Rains increase turbidity and alter water levels and currents. Wind ruffles a lake's surface and relocates baitfish. A complete list of possible changes would be long, indeed.

Here's another metaphysical law: For every action, there is a reaction. Again, applied to fishing, every change in conditions elicits some new response from bass. Changing conditions spur these fish to shift locations, to feed or quit feeding, to depend on different senses to locate and catch prey, etc.

The angler is the third link in this chain. When conditions change and bass respond, a fisherman must likewise adjust his locations and/or tactics if he is to keep getting bites.

This is a simple concept, and applying it means the difference between steak and bologna to full-time pros like Kentucky's Mike Auten.

"On the Tournament Trail, you *have* to be able to interpret changes and adapt to them. I mean, this is a matter of survival," Auten states. "I don't think I've ever fished a tournament from practice through the last competition day when conditions didn't change. And usually, the person who reacts to changes the quickest and in the most appropriate way walks off with the winner's check."

This wisdom applies to fish-for-fun anglers as well as touring professionals. Bass don't care who's pulling a bait. If it's presented in the right place with the proper allure, they'll bite Joe Schmoe's spinnerbait or

(Opposite page) A SUDDEN drop in barometric pressure sounds the dinner bell for bass prior to a frontal passage.

Windblown Banks

■ **Type of lake** — River-run reservoir in the mid-South.
■ **Features** — Extensive flooded buckbrush, stumpfields and occasional patches of vegetation.
■ **Time of year** — Fall.
■ **Best pattern** — Success this time of year is dependent on the weather. Stable, warm conditions can lead to excellent fishing. Cold temperatures and north winds yield the reverse. Cast small crankbaits along main lake gravel points, where smallmouth, largemouth, and spotted bass collect in schools to feed on shad. Also, concentrate on points exposed to moderate current and/or wind, which collects baitfish along the shore. On sunny, calm days, try topwaters around main lake stumps and logs.
■ **Key to success** — Shad must be present on a point for bass to be there in numbers.

worm as readily as Mike Auten's. Recognizing changes in fishing conditions fosters picking the right baits and retrieves. Following is a list of condition changes which anglers encounter most frequently and Auten's experience-backed advice for adjusting to them.

COLD FRONTS

This weather phenomenon is the nemesis of all bass anglers. Just prior to a frontal passage, fishing can be red hot. Then the wind shifts direction, the clouds blow away, and the needle on the barometer starts back up. When these changes occur, bass normally quit feeding. Spots, lures and methods that were yielding frequent bites suddenly become abortive. A cold frontal passage is particularly calamitous in the spring when bass are in shallow spawning areas.

"Usually, ahead of a front when the barometer is low, the fish are active, and you use aggressive baits to catch them," Auten notes. "But once the front goes by, the strike zone shrinks, and the bass become lethargic. Many of them 'bury up' in heavy cover.

"I react to this by putting the aggressive baits away and changing to a jig-and-pig. Now you have to fish much slower and more methodically, and a jig and a flipping or pitching presentation allows for this."

After a front passes, Auten turns to treetops, brushpiles, grassbeds, docks and other cover. He continues, "The trick is to work these spots slowly and thoroughly. You have to put the bait right in front of the fish and give it plenty of time to strike."

Auten is very deliberate in this process.

"If I'm fishing a brushpile or a treetop, I focus on the part with the thickest limbs," he explains.

"When flipping docks, I work the most inaccessible spots that have some cover in the water, like pilings or cross braces. When fishing grass, I drop my jig into small holes within flipping range of the edge of this green cover."

MUDDY WATER

Muddy water is a radical condition. It inhibits light penetration so much that bass have difficulty seeing their prey. Rather than deal with this situation, Auten seeks to avoid it.

"I stay away from fresh mud if possible," he says. "After a hard rain, mud washes into the creeks or upstream areas of a lake. So I'll run downstream to find cleaner water. Also, I'll lean more to fishing the main section of the lake. If I've been working a shallow pattern, I'll check out small pockets along the main lake. These don't get as much runoff as the bigger creeks, and they'll usually be the last places to get muddy."

If, however, Auten is forced to fish muddy water, he alters his tactics accordingly. "Bass pull into thick, shallow cover in muddy water, so I'll flip a jig or fish a big chartreuse spinnerbait in likely spots," he instructs. "On the spinnerbait, I'll use a large single blade that makes a lot of vibration, something like a No. 5 or 6 Colorado or Indiana. Gold is my favorite blade color for heavy mud."

WIND

When wind kicks up, feeding action may do likewise, or it might go slack, depending on the season. Auten says wind and the resultant surface agitation activates bass in summer and fall. On the other hand, it can put a damper on feeding activity in late winter and spring.

"In summer and fall, shorelines and shallow flats exposed to strong winds are excellent spots to fish," he says. "Waves stir oxygen into the water, and they move baitfish into ambush spots. Also, they break up the water surface and diffuse sunlight, so the fish are more prone to be up shallow, feeding."

In this situation, he searches out windblown banks and points with deep water nearby, especially those with riprap and chunk rocks. He seines these areas with aggressive lures like spinnerbaits, jerkbaits and shallow diving crankbaits.

IF THE WATER LEVEL where you are fishing is rising or falling, throw a medium diving crankbait at the new contours created by the altered water level.

"Another pattern I like in the wind is fishing grassbeds," he notes. "I start on the upwind side of a grassbed and let the breeze blow me across it. While I'm drifting, I watch for holes and points in the grass, which are natural ambush spots. I fish these with a spinnerbait or a buzzbait, if the waves aren't too high."

RISING OR FALLING WATER

Fluctuating water levels definitely affect bass locations. When a lake level jumps up, bass move into freshly flooded areas. When the level falls, they pull back to points and banks close to deep sanctuaries.

"If a lake is rising, I'll concentrate on fishing green bushes, weeds or any other similar cover," he says. "One of my favorite patterns for this condition is hitting pockets along the sides of the creeks. I fish as far back in them as I can get. Bass are usually in these areas to chase food, so a spinnerbait or a buzzbait are top lure picks.

"On the other hand, when the lake is falling, I'll move to points near the creek mouth or out on the main lake. Also, I might try pockets in the lower

ends of the creeks, focusing on the point cover. In either case, having deep water close by is the key."

Good lure presentations for this condition include slow rolling spinnerbaits and fishing different contours with medium diving crankbaits or Carolina rigged worms or lizards.

CURRENTS

Increased water flow usually incites bass to feed. It steers bait into predictable areas, so the predator fish collect on these spots for the banquet. This can be true in both reservoir and tailwater situations.

"A good example of this is on power generation lakes, such as Kentucky Lake, where I live," Auten points out. "When current is slack, bass spread out and feed randomly. But when the generators come on and the current kicks up, they school on such structure as points, ledges bordering shallow flats, channel intersections and other places where the flow washes baitfish by. This is one of the best situations you can find. Those bass are there to eat, and if you can get a bait in front of them, they'll bite it." Aggressive baits that imitate shad are the best lures here. Diving and lipless crankbaits are the standards.

FOLLOWING SPRING-TIME frontal passages, stow the reaction baits, slow down, and use baits that can be worked methodically through prespawn staging areas.

NEITHER RAIN NOR SNOW

Learn how the pros cope with the worst weather

DEAN ROJAS HAD MADE A GOOD cast to send his jig far underneath the boat dock, but when a bass hit the lure, Rojas missed the strike. It had been sleeting since just after dawn and Rojas' hands were so cold he couldn't grasp the reel handle.

At Lake Shasta, a cold, driving rain began before dawn and continued the entire day. High winds turned Lake Mead into a frothing ocean of 5-foot waves and whitecaps. Storms across Lake Eufaula caused the water to rise 7 feet in two days.

If you're getting the idea professional tournament bass fishing is not quite the fair-weather sport many think it is, you're right. In the course of a typical BASS tournament season that continues from July to the following May and stretches from California to Vermont and south Florida to the Canadian border, weather conditions will range from perfect to good to bad to worse — and the pros will fish through nearly all of them.

"In many instances, the weather is so bad that simply taking care of yourself becomes a major priority," says Rojas, who holds the BASS record for heaviest winning weight at 108 pounds, 12 ounces. "The challenge of catching fish becomes much more mental than physical. You try to block out the conditions and concentrate on fishing, but it's hard."

"The weather is probably the one element that equalizes everyone in this sport when it turns really bad," adds fellow pro Ron Shuffield. "No one likes to fish under adverse conditions, but when you have to, you try to keep in mind that conditions are miserable for everyone.

"As Dean says, that makes it a thinking game, and I personally enjoy those kinds of challenges."

In more than a dozen years on the pro tour, Shuffield has gained a reputation as one to watch when the weather turns bad. As a prime example, he won a major BASS title on Nashville's Old Hickory Lake during a week that saw water levels move up and down the scale like a yo-yo.

His most notable bad weather win, however, took place during a November competition held on Oklahoma's Grand Lake. Air temperatures seldom climbed above freezing the entire week and usually hovered closer to 20 degrees. Shuffield led all three days and finished with an astounding 49 pounds, 1 ounce.

"I was wearing insulated underwear, regular tournament shirt and blue jeans, a down jacket,

FISHING IN the flakes requires a slower presentation and recognizing the fish will hold tight to cover, like boat docks.

a snowmobile suit, gloves, and a full toboggan," the Arkansas pro remembers. "I felt like the Michelin Man out there, but at least I did stay warm."

Although Rojas has fished in extremely cold weather himself, a tournament with totally different weather conditions — wind — stands out as one of the worst in his memory. "I was fishing Lake Mead," he remembers, "and coming back to Callville Bay for weigh-in.

"I'd been fishing protected water, so I didn't realize how hard the wind was blowing or how rough the lake had become. When I came out of the Narrows, I was met head-on by a wall of water and big waves. It's normally only a 10 minute run from there to the marina, but it took over an hour under those conditions."

Timing Is Everything

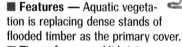

■ **Type of lake** — Large mainstream reservoir in the South.
■ **Features** — Aquatic vegetation is replacing dense stands of flooded timber as the primary cover.
■ **Time of year** — Midwinter.
■ **Best pattern** — January brings the coldest weather of the year to the South, and bass can be fickle. The best fishing comes after three warm days in a row or after a warm rain. In either condition, head to the backs of the creeks and fish a 1/2-ounce spinnerbait over adjacent humps and flats. Typical depths are 5 to 15 feet over the channel and less than 5 feet on bordering structure.
■ **Key to success** — Timing is important. Fish these shallow areas in the warmest part of the day — midafternoon. This is when bass will be most active.

Strategies
For Windy Days

What really happens to the lake and its bass when the wind blows? Plenty, Capt. Ray Van Horn has found. Van Horn doubles as a guide on the windswept inland bass lakes of Florida and on the coast for the finny denizens of the deep. Here's what he has to say when you have no other choice but to face the wind.

■ Wind shakes up shallow and emergent vegetation — "Wind creates wave action that moves submerged vegetation around, especially in water less than 4 feet deep. This dislodges minute food particles from the grass, attracting minnows and immature fish, which in turn draw in predators like bass. Insects are often dislodged from emergent grasses like maidencane, creating a similar feeding scenario."

■ Wind oxygenates the water — "This can be especially important in a reservoir in hot weather, where dissolved oxygen may be alarmingly low. More oxygen means more active fish."

■ Wind creates currents — "Wind currents are often overlooked as bass-positioning factors. Strong winds can create extremely strong currents, especially through necked-down areas — such as between the main shoreline and an island."

■ Wind repositions plankton — "Plankton blooms near the surface, where sunlight is the most intense. These blooms drift in the direction of the wind, where they are targeted by shad."

■ Wind reduces light penetration — "Wave action created by strong breezes cuts down on light penetration. This can have an adverse effect when fishing live bait, since the fish can't see the offering as well. But when fishing lures, this is usually a positive, for it helps disguise the inherent flaws or unrealistic features of the lure's design."

■ Wind can alter water temperatures — "Sometimes large masses of warm water are literally repositioned to another part of the lake after several days of strong winds. A cold north wind can likewise lower the lake's temperature overnight."

■ Wind creates color edges — "Bass are attracted to places where one type of habitat changes into another — like a mudline. Color edges are common on windy lakes, where silted water may form a line against clear water."

■ Wind repositions bass — "In general, I've found that bass range farther from cover in windy areas, and often move shallower."

One thing wind does NOT do, Van Horn emphasizes, is blow baitfish around. "This myth is so pervasive, even some of the most competent bass pros believe it," Van Horn points out. "A healthy baitfish is not capable of being blown anywhere by anything short of a hurricane. A dying shad struggling on the surface may indeed be blown with the wind, but not a school of bait."

Van Horn attributes this mistaken notion to the fact that baitfish — and bass — are often thick on windy banks. "But this happens mainly because plankton blooms drift to these windy banks. The minnows, in turn, move in to feed on the plankton, and the bass follow."

Sometimes, inclement weather causes tournament officials to cancel a competition day. Leisure anglers can equate that scenario to getting rained out of a fishing trip for the day.

"Loss of a fishing day means you have that much less time to figure out patterns and catch fish," says Rojas. "Very often in a three day event, you may not have everything really figured out until the third day, and you can bring in a really big catch and move up in the standings. When you lose a day of competition, you also lose that opportunity."

With these thoughts in mind, here's a quick look at how pros like Rojas and Shuffield still catch bass when the weather does turn upside down during a tournament:

SWELTERING HEAT

"For personal safety, I drink a lot of liquids during the day, including at least a pint of water before I ever start fishing," says Rojas, who knows from experience after having lived at Lake Havasu, where the temperature in the Arizona desert reaches 100 degrees.

"Technique-wise, in the clear water of many Western lakes, the faster you can retrieve a lure like a spinnerbait, the better the fish will hit it. I try to cover a lot of water, concentrating in off-lake pockets around rocks and brush, and especially around any shade I can find.

"On lakes like Havasu and Powell, I like to use a big topwater lure like a Zara Spook, too. If you retrieve it fast but still make a lot of noise, you can bring bass up from 12 to 15 feet deep to hit it."

"In Southern lakes, the hot weather technique we use most often is quite different," notes Shuffield. "We may have topwater action around dawn, but after that, we do better by fishing jigs or giant plastic worms around brush or outside grass lines in 10 to 20 feet of water, and we work the lures extremely slow.

"I find a lot of fish suspended in extremely hot conditions, often over points or breaklines, but they're still active fish that usually hit a lure on the initial fall."

EXTREME COLD

"When I won at Grand Lake, my reel was freezing every second or third cast," remembers

Shuffield. "That meant I was not making nearly as many presentations as I normally would, so I had to make sure each cast I did make went exactly where I wanted it, and then I had to work each retrieve as carefully and as exacting as I could.

"Those were the problems. I found bass hold-ing in less than 8 feet of water, and when the fish did hit, they hit solidly. The key for nearly all cold weather fishing is to fish very slowly and stay around cover. I like to fish boat docks, especially those closer to the mouths of creeks, with a jig. If grass is present underwater, I'll often slow

BE ON the water at sunrise to take advantage of the brief window of opportunity when the topwater bite is hot during summertime.

roll a heavy spinnerbait down right over the top of it."

"Another technique that often works well in cold weather is to fish current," notes Rojas. "Some bass probably live in current throughout the year, and those fish are accustomed to the colder temperature. If you can fish jigs or soft plastics in the eddies formed behind rocks or logs in the current, you'll generally pick up some fish. I also like to fish crankbaits or slow spinnerbaits along rocks and riprap close to current."

FLUCTUATING WATER

"I love falling water," smiles Rojas, "because it seems to move bass to deeper pockets where they gather in groups. You can catch two or three fish from places like this on a crankbait, then return an hour later and catch several more.

"Falling water also seems to move bass tighter to cover, where a jig or plastic worm becomes more effective. Sometimes it's necessary to downsize your lures under these conditions just to give the fish something different to look at."

"The basic rule for rising water is that bass move shallow," continues Shuffield, "and I believe that holds true. The fish do not necessarily always come up to the 'new' shoreline, however. Very often bass will suspend in or very close to bushes and trees near the 'old' shoreline. They also tend to

Quick Tips
For Success In The Wind

■ Cast into the wind, retrieve with the wind — Don't argue — just do it! Your strikes will increase threefold.

■ Avoid finesse lures and presentations — Use lures you can cast into the wind, artificials heavy enough to feel. Crankbaits, lipless vibrating lures, Carolina rigged worms and spinnerbaits work best.

■ Fish shallower — Bass can move amazingly shallow on windswept banks and points.

■ Target offshore structure — From postspawn to fall, humps, weedbeds and big flats are best. Drifting plankton blooms will draw schools of bait, and bass will follow.

■ Fish funnels — "Neckdowns," where current is intensified, can be your key to the heaviest bass limit of your fishing career.

■ Try topwaters — Don't laugh — a noisy propeller plug or buzzbait can catch the lunker of a lifetime on a windy day!

be more scattered so that you don't catch more than one bass from a single target.

"This is when pitching or flipping a plastic worm or grub to the cover and slowly swimming it back out often works extremely well. If the lake you're fishing has a lot of deeper weedbeds, the fish will sometimes move right over the vegetation, and you can catch them with a buzzbait or spinnerbait."

WINDBLOWN

"Wind affects boat and lure control more than fishing," explains Rojas, "so the best remedy is to try to find calm water. This can be in a cove, behind a point, or sometimes up a tributary creek.

"Once out of the wind, you can look at what cover options the bass have and fish accordingly. I like to fish spinnerbaits around rocks or brush in the backs of coves, or pitch a plastic worm or tube jig to isolated stickups.

"In open water but close to cover, topwater lures like buzzbaits and Spooks may do surprisingly well, especially in clear lakes."

RAIN AND SNOW

"One of the most surprising lures for snow is often a buzzbait," says Shuffield, who has used one several times when fishing in the flakes. He has no idea why it works, but it seems to be a good pattern only when the water has warmed for several days or weeks and then turns cold again very suddenly.

"In the rain, spinnerbaits are often good around boat docks, weedbeds and other cover," he continues. "If thunderstorms and lightning have been rumbling through an area for several hours, however, the fishing is usually pretty poor. I'm not sure what causes this, either, because fishing is sometimes really good just before a storm.

"I like to fish windy points or brushlines with a crankbait, or work docks and boathouses with a jig or

plastic worm when it's raining. That way, if the rain gets really bad and lightning starts flashing, I'm close to cover.

"Even though most of us regularly fish in bad weather, we still like to get out of it occasionally, too."

IF HEAT IS ON the menu for your fishing day, tie on a large Zara Spook. Bass like to get a lot of bang for their buck when they expend energy in the summer, and the walking bait is a mouthful.

THE PRESENCE of shad is a common thread in the winning strategies of most bass tournaments.

UNDERSTANDING BAITFISH MOVEMENTS

Find the bait, and you'll find the bass

WHEN ROBERT HAMILTON WON the 1992 Bassmaster Classic on Alabama's Logan Martin Lake, it wasn't — as many believe — due to using the perfect lure or finding the perfect structure. It wasn't even due to perfect luck.

Instead, Hamilton attributes his world championship to a tiny, silvery white fish named *Dorosoma petenense*, better known as the threadfin shad.

"My Classic win was almost totally dependent on shad," remembers Hamilton. "I could ride over the underwater structure I was fishing and see the shad on my depthfinder. When the baitfish were scattered, even though they were near the surface, I never caught any bass.

"It was only when the shad began to bunch tightly and hold deeper — 7 or 8 feet over the top of the structure — that I'd catch anything. The shad were so thick at times I couldn't even see the bottom, but those were the times bass started feeding.

"After the first day of seeing this, I wouldn't even stay in the area to fish unless the shad were like this."

Fast-forward a year, to the 1993 Classic on the same lake. Hamilton's shad never showed up, and his deeper structure holes never produced.

(Opposite page) SHAD INFLUENCED the world championship winning strategy of Robert Hamilton. David Fritts, his successor to the title one year later on the same fishery, also relied on this favored prey of the largemouth.

In contrast, winner David Fritts worked shallow structure and underwater cover, keying on underwater targets and — you guessed it — shad. At each place Fritts found and caught bass, he also saw plenty of baitfish activity.

Search Out Suspended Bait

■ **Type of lake** — Western water storage reservoir.

■ **Features** — Small canyon impoundment known for huge bass.

■ **Time of year** — Midsummer.

■ **Best pattern** — Early in the morning, head to the upper end of the lake and cast surface lures, jerkbaits and swim baits around baitfish pods. The baitfish can be seen on the surface or spotted with a depthfinder. They typically suspend over 15 to 30 feet of water, and schools of bass follow them. Cast topwaters and jerkbaits to any surface feeding activity. If the baitfish are down, drop a swim bait to their level before starting a steady swimming retrieve.

■ **Key to success** — The presence of baitfish is a must. If minnows aren't present in big numbers, bass won't be there either.

Shad Facts

These facts about threadfin and gizzard shad should help you home in on shad-eating bass.

■ **Distribution** — Gizzard shad were originally distributed throughout much of the eastern two-thirds of the United States, with the exceptions of North Dakota, northern Minnesota, Wisconsin, the Appalachians, northern New England and southern Florida. Their range has been extended now into Wyoming and south Florida.

The original range of the threadfin shad extended from Kentucky and southern Indiana across the South to Mexico. They have successfully been introduced into California, the Rocky Mountain West, Nebraska, Illinois and Missouri.

■ **Age** — Gizzard shad can live as long as 10 to 13 years; the normal age limit is about seven years. Threadfin only live three or four years.

■ **Size** — Gizzard shad can reach lengths of over 16 inches and may weigh nearly 1 1/2 pounds. Threadfin rarely exceed 7 inches. The largest threadfin ever reported measured 8.1 inches and came from the Bogue Falaya River in Louisiana.

■ **Reproduction** — Female gizzard shad often contain eggs of different diameters. The large eggs are spawned first, the smaller ones weeks later, after they mature. A single female may spawn 500,000 eggs at a time.

■ **Temperature Tolerance** — Both gizzard and threadfin are susceptible to thermal stress in cold water. Threadfin are the most temperature-sensitive and cannot survive water temperatures of 39 degrees or less.

■ **Identification** — Both shad are silvery white in color and have distinctly forked tails. The threadfin's tail has a yellow tinge while the gizzard shad's tail does not. The lower jaw of the threadfin projects beyond the tip of the snout, but a gizzard shad has a blunt nose, and the jaw does not project beyond it. The threadfin receives its name from the last ray of its dorsal fin, which flows out over the spine like a thread. The gizzard shad, however, also has the same configuration. The gizzard shad receives its name from the fact it actually has a gizzard, while a threadfin does not.

"The two types of shad in our impoundments, threadfin and the gizzard shad (*Dorosoma cepedianum*), can have profound impacts on the entire aquatic ecosystem because they are such important foods — not only for bass, but also for many other species," says fishery scientist Dr. Loren Hill.

"Robert Hamilton and David Fritts are not the first anglers to win tournaments because of shad. The majority of bass tournaments, except for those held during the spring spawning season, can be attributed in some part to the presence of threadfin or gizzard shad. Most anglers just don't realize it."

Those are important words of praise for two fish about which the fisheries community has done little official research. Enough is known, however, to realize that the well-being of sportfish populations depends on threadfin and gizzard shad.

Shad, of course, are not the only food on the bass menu. Because bass are such opportunistic feeders, their diet includes such diverse items as crawfish, bluegill and other small sunfish, frogs, baby ducks, rainbow trout and even their own offspring. Because shad often comprise such a large proportion of the total fish population in a lake, however, they can influence the availability of these other creatures.

Although bass feed heavily on both gizzard and threadfin shad throughout most of the year, nature has its own ways of taking care of possible overpopulations of these prolific baitfish. Both species, the threadfin in particular, are especially sensitive to cold water.

In part, this temperature/stress relationship may be one of the reasons shad seem to be continually moving throughout a lake. These movements are not confined to the seasons, but in many instances are daily.

Over the years, anglers and guides have occasionally noticed these movements and been able to take advantage of them, because bass followed the shad. Professional guides on highland lakes have reported daily shad migrations that could be tracked for more than half a mile. In nearly every instance, bass follow behind and underneath the shad, feeding on them periodically.

These feeding binges appear to occur most often when the school of shad is more compressed, as it might be when it funnels along a ditch or channel, or when it rises or sinks over a ridge or other type of structure to a particular depth, as Hamilton found during his Classic win. These also happen to be natural ambush points.

"We can't pinpoint exactly what is occurring or why," says Hill, "because shad, as you can imagine, are not the easiest fish to study. They're too small for radio transmitters, and of course, they're eaten by the thousands every day.

"We do know that huge concentrations of shad will move into shallow water to seek shoreline cover during nocturnal hours. Often, it is to a mossbed, treeline or other type of vegetation; it is not simply to open, shallow water.

"Then, early in the morning, these same shad

leave and head toward deeper water, where they roam throughout the day. Shad, in fact, spend much of their lives roaming throughout a lake, but these migrations into shallow water occur daily between spring and fall.

"We see shad when they're traveling in huge schools or swarms, and from time to time, anglers encounter them, and when they do, the fishing can be fantastic. Unfortunately, the movements into and out of shallow water are not always in such visible schools. It's only when some obstacle tends to bunch the baitfish that we really notice them.

"That is why not many people really know about this movement pattern at all."

According to research conducted by Hill, shad spawn in very shallow water, over sand, gravel, wood, vegetation and even mud. Water temperatures for gizzard shad at this time can be as cold as 57 degrees or as warm as 75 degrees, so the activity normally begins as early as mid-April in parts of their range.

Threadfin shad can have multiple spawning periods between April and August, as long as the water temperature ranges between 66 and 75 degrees, which is another possible explanation for their movements to shallow water each evening.

The eggs are adhesive and stick to the first hard surface they touch. As soon as the eggs are deposited, the adults leave. Incubation for both shad species takes up to three days and, although they may hatch near shore, they don't stay there long.

"Newly hatched shad larvae gradually migrate to pelagic areas (living near the surface of open areas of the lake) as they grow," says Hill. "They range from near the surface down to the pH breakline and thermocline, but both horizontal and vertical movements can change in response to water elevation, turbidity, storms and food availability — so it's easy to see that both gizzard and threadfin shad always keep a suitcase packed."

Once shad are located, the obvious question is how to take advantage of them to catch bass. The answer to that often depends on the season of the year as well as where the shad are located.

"In late spring, I like small crankbaits," explains

Wind-Driven Current

In lakes that don't have artificial current driven by the turbines of a power generation plant, the wind can create moving water that has the same effect on bass.

"On lakes that have no traditional form of current, wind current can have a major impact on bass location and behavior," veteran Texas pro Alton Jones believes. "Wind current will congregate the fish. On Richland Chambers, my home lake, even the slightest breeze creates a fairly strong current that will cause bass to stack up on various pieces of structure a half-mile offshore.

"Typically, this current will position bass on the upwind side of the structure so they can sit on the upper edge of the dropoff. I'm thinking of a tank dam that is about 100 yards long. If there's no wind, you might catch one here and there all around it without any real rhyme or reason. But if the wind is from the south, those fish will be stacked up on the south end of the dam. If the wind is out of the north, they will be on the north end of it. It's like clockwork.

"Again, the bass are using the wind current for a strategic feeding advantage. There is something that wind current is creating that's making it an easy place for them to get a meal. Hopefully, that meal is my lizard."

Hamilton. "You fish around the school, keying on any structure or cover that may be available. You don't simply start casting through the shad.

"As summer progresses, I use larger and larger crankbaits, because the shad are getting larger. But in the autumn I switch to small crankbaits again because many of the shad are small, due to a late spawn. When bass are feeding heavily on schools of shad, sometimes 'matching the hatch' with the right size of lure is really important."

In the winter, when the water grows much colder, the shad migrate back out of the creeks and into main lake depths. On some lakes, this can easily be 40 to 60 feet deep. The fish kills occur most often in shallower lakes, or in sections of a lake that are primarily shallow, when the temperature drops quickly and then stays cold.

Although the shad continue to roam in the winter months, they generally remain in deep water because of their temperature tolerances. Gradually, as the water warms in early spring, they begin to move shallow and adhere to the in-and-out daily movement cycle.

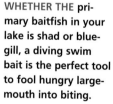

WHETHER THE primary baitfish in your lake is shad or bluegill, a diving swim bait is the perfect tool to fool hungry largemouth into biting.

WEEKDAYS VS. WEEKENDS

Here's how to win the weekend water wars
on busy bass lakes

IT'S WEDNESDAY MORNING at a well-known bass lake as you launch at a practically deserted boat ramp. You glide over slick water to a nearby cove and approach a fallen tree, the most obvious piece of cover along the entire bank. Your first cast of the morning goes astray; your spinnerbait sails 6 feet wide of the tree's trunk. You

briskly wind in with the intention of making a better cast, but a respectable bass pounces on the lure.

You chuckle, release the suicidal fish and lay the next cast right along the trunk. Pow! Bass No. 2 nails your spinnerbait. Throughout the morning, your spinnerbait dances past windfalls, brushpiles, boat docks and other visible targets and coaxes strikes

with satisfying regularity. You later head home, reassured that you are one heck of a fisherman, and that your favorite lake supports a bounty of bass.

The following Saturday, you impatiently wait in a long line at the same boat ramp. You finally get on the water and bounce over boat wakes to the cove you fished the previous weekday, heart set on starting at the same fallen tree. When you get there, a pair of anglers in another boat is already working over *your* tree.

The rest of the day is equally frustrating. Many spots that produced during midweek refuse to give up bass to your trusty spinnerbait. At day's end, you find yourself arm-weary despite catching few fish. You leave, doubting your skills and wondering if this could possibly be the same lake you fished only days before.

Bass fishing ranks have swelled to the point that popular lakes exhibit dual personalities, one for weekdays and another for weekends. As a result, we must deal with schizoid bass that often strike with abandon Monday through Friday, yet grow tightlipped when fishing's working masses venture out on Saturday.

This phenomenon is something professional tournament anglers and fishing guides have coped with for years — some more successfully than others. Now that bass anglers, as a whole, grow increasingly capable, it's more important than ever that you adjust your fishing according to the day of the week.

TAKE A RIDE

Texan David Wharton, an established BASS professional and former Sam Rayburn guide,

sometimes avoids the weekend crush by making long runs from popular boat launching facilities.

"When I was guiding," says Wharton, "the wind was my ally. Most people won't go far when the lake gets rough. If I was willing to ride the big water and cross Rayburn, I could get into areas away from ramps and leave most people behind."

Under normal conditions, however, Wharton's primary strategy is to fish structure in open water. He correctly reasons that the majority of weekend warriors concentrate on shallow, visible cover. Fishing offshore, he points out, doesn't necessarily mean fishing deep.

"If you want to fish shallow," says Wharton, "check out creek channels in the backs of creeks. That way you don't have to beat the banks along with everybody else."

Wharton's most productive offshore spots have been places he has located himself. Even though most fishermen are more comfortable fishing the bank and visible cover, "community holes" away from shore also get pounded on weekends. A tip regarding a hot structure spot may yield good fishing during the week, but will likely be overrun on weekends, just as with shoreline cover.

In The Cool Of The Night

■ **Type of lake** — Large mainstream reservoir in the South.
■ **Features** — Aquatic vegetation is replacing dense stands of flooded timber as the primary cover.
■ **Time of year** — Midsummer.
■ **Best pattern** — The weather is scorching-hot and pleasure boaters are out in droves. As a result, some of the best fishing occurs at night, especially just before and just after a full moon. Bass burrow into thick hydrilla beds in the daytime, but they come out at night to feed. Fish a black spinnerbait on a steady retrieve, or hop Texas rigged worms along the bottom next to the hydrilla edges.
■ **Key to success** — Deep water must be present. Don't fish a hydrilla line unless the depth drops just out from the vegetation.

Fishing
In A Crowd

Fish enough weekend days, and there will be times when you will be fishing around other anglers competing for the same bass.

While most of us relate fishing with solitude, there is a real art to fishing in a crowd. One of the best pros at dealing with this intimidating situation is BASS superstar Larry Nixon.

"It doesn't bother me to fish in a crowd," Nixon says. "As long as I have the right cover available — something invisible like submerged vegetation or an underwater bar — I can handle fishing around other people. If you take the proper approach and keep a good attitude, you can catch fish in the middle of other fishermen.

"The one thing I hate about fishing in a crowd is that there are times when the people fishing the same area will spook the fish. They might be banging on all of the cover, running a noisy trolling motor on high-24 and just churning up the area. That's the thing that frustrates me and makes me pick up my trolling motor and get the heck out of there."

An example of Nixon's ability to stand out in a crowd came during a famed MegaBucks tournament on Florida's Harris Chain.

Nixon spent much of the tournament fishing a plastic worm in a large lily pad field known as the Bryant Park area, a stretch of pads that produced an estimated 2,000 bass during that tournament. But Nixon took a different approach, one that resulted in seven bass averaging more than 3 pounds apiece. While most of the other pros were fishing subtle lures like plastic worms and lizards, Nixon chunked a medium running crankbait.

"The key was using something different and reading the cover correctly," he explains. "There were a lot of lily pads, a lot of scattered clumps and some individual stalks. The area has a million different casting angles. I was able to find casting angles different from the rest of the crowd."

Nixon offers these additional tips for fishing in a crowd:

■ The proper mental approach — "Ignore everybody and just concentrate on being more efficient than the others. The biggest mistake people make is worrying about everybody else and not concentrating. In a crowded situation, it is important to concentrate on each cast and each retrieve. The guy who bears down and maintains his concentration is the one who will succeed."

■ Be observant — "Keep your eyes open and watch for areas that are getting a little rest — places where nobody is in there fooling with the fish. Slip into that spot and fish it."

■ Watch others — "It pays to be observant of what other people are doing. If everybody else is flipping, you need to be casting. In that case, I'm going to cover a lot of water and make more casts than anyone.

"On the other hand, if the people around you are doing the right thing and everybody is catching fish, analyze what they are doing and try to duplicate it."

If you can locate your own offshore bass, chances are good that you'll have them to yourself. This strategy came though for Wharton when he once competed in a BASS tournament held at South Carolina's Lake Murray, which he had never fished before. Fortunately for Wharton, Murray has submergent vegetation, something he is accustomed to fishing at Rayburn. Rather than pump local anglers for locations of their productive grassbeds, Wharton set out with a topographic map and a depthfinder.

He eventually located a 200-yard stretch of weeds in 10 to 12 feet of water on a long point. The grass grew up 4 to 5 feet from the bottom and was easy to overlook. Best of all, there wasn't another angler in the vicinity. When Wharton slow rolled a spinnerbait over the weeds and plucked a number of quality bass, he had an inkling he was on to something good.

On four consecutive tournament days, including the final round on Saturday, Wharton fished his weedbed in solitude. The fishing was slow but steady as the weeds eventually gave up 48 pounds, 12 ounces of bass, enough poundage for first place.

LOOSE LIPS SINK SHIPS

Another thing Wharton has learned about overcoming weekend anglers *and* fellow tournament competitors is to keep a good thing to himself. He never let on exactly where he was fishing at Murray. Two years later he returned to the lake for another tournament and keyed on the same weedbed. He won the tournament hands down by fishing the same area as before. Had he revealed the spot after the initial event, local weekend anglers would have fished it dry.

Mike Auten, who guided on Kentucky Lake until he began making an impact on the professional BASS trail, also knows how to keep mum.

"A lot of structure fishing goes on at Kentucky Lake," says Auten. "It's hard to keep your best spots to yourself. When I found something really good, I never fished it on weekends, especially if it was something I had developed by planting cover. All it takes is for one guy to see you fishing a secret spot. Before you know it, everybody is fishing there."

THE WEEKDAY BOOM

Of course, Auten also took his clients to community structure holes that were visited regularly by other anglers, as well as to shallow cover. He

learned early in his guiding career that well-known structures yielded far more bass on weekdays than on weekends, the same as with shoreline cover.

"After a weekend of heavy fishing," says Auten, "it takes a few days for the bass to come around. Along about midweek, things really pick up. Then the weekend masses hit the water and the cycle begins all over again."

The weekday vs. weekend cycle taught Auten to be wary when prefishing tournaments. Professional and amateur competitors alike often overrate the places they find when scouting on weekdays. This trap is particularly hard on those who take a day off during the week to prepare for a weekend tournament.

Because weekday bass are more aggressive, they may fill you with unrealistic expectations. Unless you are fairly certain you've found water that will be overlooked, you must anticipate the effects additional fishing pressure will have when the weekend rolls around. In most instances, you'll have to share the bass with other anglers, and the fish may

be much less cooperative.

The truth is, you may be ahead if you can prefish a weekend tournament on the weekend preceding the event. You probably won't catch as many bass as on weekdays, but you will see which areas receive the most fishing pressure and which lures and presentations get the most play. Given this information, you then have an opportunity to search for overlooked fishing water and to come up with alternative methods the bass haven't seen countless times.

"When I fish on weekends," says Auten, "I try to beat everybody to the best spots first. But that rarely works. I've had better luck trying to show the bass something different from what everybody else is throwing. What I really need to do is work harder at finding less obvious spots."

MOST WEEKEND anglers will be flinging their favorite spinnerbait or worm all day long. So, when fishing pressure is heavy, throw a bait that other fishermen fail to consider and that bass have not seen.

ICE-OUT BASS
Early bass season action can be hot on Northern lakes

ICE-OUT smallmouth relate to bluffs so they can move vertically in the water column. Changing weather conditions force smallmouth to move vertically in the water column, making bluffs primary structure during ice-out.

I T'S A SECRET that some in-the-know Northern bass anglers do not want to share. At a time of the year when they practically have the lake to themselves, why would they want things to change by encouraging others to join them?

Fortunately, a few bass experts are not so selfish and are willing to talk about it. What's the secret? Largemouth bass fishing is fantastic at "ice-out."

Among many Northern anglers there is a false assumption that it takes weeks for largemouth to "move in" from deeper water or that the lake must warm to nearly 50 degrees before bass turn on. The truth is, bass are shallow and feeding much earlier than most anglers imagine.

But it is very easy to completely miss this ice-out action. There are plenty of opportunities for

mistakes. You'll miss it if you fish the wrong area . . . or the wrong bait . . . or even the right lure at the wrong speed.

However, if you do things right, the reward can be some of the most exciting bass fishing of the entire season.

NO WAITING PERIOD

If you have ever spent a winter snowbound up North, then you understand the malady known as Cabin Fever. Northern anglers often talk about how anxious they are for the ice to melt so they can start fishing. Yet when open water becomes available, suddenly there is reluctance on their part to get on the water. They tinker with tackle, wash and wax the boat, even rake the yard. All that time, they're waiting for the water to reach the magic temperature they think is necessary for bass to begin their spring feeding activity.

"There is no need to wait once the ice melts," insists Ohio pro Frank Scalish. "This isn't like impoundment fishing in the South, where bass seem to take their time moving from wintering grounds to the shallows. In the North Country, things happen quickly after ice-out. Perhaps this is due to the shorter growing season; maybe bass instinctively know they must act at the first hint of warming water. Bass are shallow and looking for food almost immediately after ice-out. I'll start catching them in 6 feet of water on breaklines. I've even caught bass by pulling my jig into the water from a ring of ice frozen around the bases of shoreline bushes."

Fellow Ohio pro Jeff Snyder concurs.

"If Northern bass anglers sit back and wait for textbook situations, they will miss some of the most interesting fishing of the year," says Snyder. "If you know the right areas and the right baits to use, it is possible to catch bass on artificial lures in some very chilly water."

According to both Scalish and Snyder, the "right area" must have a food supply and be warmer than other shallow water in the lake. It's the warmer water that triggers early spring algae and plankton blooms in the shallows. That attracts baitfish, which in turn draws bass to these sites.

"I'm not afraid to be fishing in the mud at ice-out," says Scalish. "Some of those shallow, black bottom areas warm quickly under a bright sun. If there is grass in the lake, then so much the better. I'll choose the shallowest grassline in a protected bay or cove — preferably on the northwest side of the lake.

"And I want a distinct channel or ditch running through the bay. It need not be a big channel. Actually, a drop of only 2 or 3 feet is sufficient. But that ditch or channel is paramount to bass movement at ice-out. Given the unpredictable weather in the spring, those shallow bass will have a spot to drop back to if temperatures plummet."

Protected Water

- **Type of lake** — Lowland reservoir in the East.
- **Features** — Average depth is less than 10 feet; grassbeds and cypress stumps are the two main types of cover.
- **Time of year** — Late winter.
- **Best pattern** — Head to the lower portion of the lake and flip or pitch a 3/8- to 1/2-ounce jig-and-pig around cypress trees. Home in on coves and bays that are shielded from a north wind. Flip into cypress knees and between clusters of trees. Use heavy tackle, since the likelihood of hooking a heavy bass is high.
- **Key to success** — Find out the direction of the prevailing wind for the previous three days, and concentrate on areas that have been shielded from this wind.

tions that dam breasts and midlake causeways are not the sort of riprap that draws bass at ice-out. Instead, look for protected areas such as elevated roadbeds in the backs of bays, marinas with riprap banks and similar situations. He also insists that a dropoff be close to the rocks. He believes the dropoff is needed for the same reason Scalish looks for a channel — bass must be able to retreat to slightly deeper water without making a long migration across an exceptionally shallow bay.

ICE-OUT TECHNIQUES

Each angler has a small "must-have" list of baits for the ice-out frenzy. At first glance, their choices seem like standard bass fishing fare. But upon closer examination, each has tailored the baits for coldwater presentations.

Snyder opts for a jig-and-pig as his No. 1 pick. He uses a small profile jig of his own design coupled with a medium pork frog trailer. He insists that the jig skirt be living rubber as opposed to the newer silicone skirts. According to Snyder, rubber is more reactive to the subtle lure movements he uses in cold water.

Because the pickups are so subtle at this time, Snyder advises every angler to be a line watcher. "Chances are you are not going to feel a coldwater bite. I focus my attention on where the line enters the water. It's like looking at a bobber; if you watch it closely, you can see line movement that indicates a bass has picked up the bait," he says.

Snyder backs up his jig-and-pig with two other early spring favorites: a willowleaf spin-

Snyder also has specific prerequisites for early spring fishing. "I want some type of rock in the shallows," he says. "When rock is exposed to the sun and protected from the open lake, it acts as a solar collector, heating up during the day and radiating that absorbed heat back into the water after the sun goes down. This helps create a warmer environment for a longer period of time each day, thereby stimulating algae growth."

According to Snyder, riprap shorelines are perfect, but he cau-

WHEN THE WEATHER is cold and the bass are finicky, Frank Scalish opts for a Shad Rap — especially if shallow grass is present. When the trebles snag the vegetation, he rips the lure free, usually causing lethargic bass to bite.

nerbait and a supershallow crankbait. "A slow rolled Pro Model Spinnerbait from Wacko Tackle is my 'go-to' lure when the wind is blowing against a productive bank," he says. "A 9 1/2-pounder, the heaviest Ohio largemouth I've ever taken, came on a spinnerbait during the ice-out period."

Just the opposite weather condition brings the Mann's 1-Minus crankbait out of the box, Snyder notes. "When the sun is bright and the wind is dead-calm, bass sometimes rise near the surface on very shallow flats to bask in the warmth. That's when I slow crank the 1-Minus."

Scalish has a lineup of similar baits for the ice-out period. His picks include a jig-and-pig, spinnerbait and tight-wobble crankbait. "I pretty much live or die with these baits," he says. "I don't get crazy with a lot of lures. It just isn't necessary."

A custom-made 1/4-ounce jig with a skirt of hair and living rubber is Scalish's special bait. And like Snyder, he tips his jig with a medium-size Super Pork frog.

"Some people have the idea that you need to fish small baits in the North when the water is cold, but don't believe it," says Scalish. "The truth is, baitfish have not spawned yet. All the shad and shiners are mature during this time, and that is what bass are expecting to feed on. In the late spring and early summer when baitfish are hatching, then you can make a case for small lures — but not at ice-out."

His spinnerbait of choice for ice-out is a Terminator T2 with turtleback blades," advises Scalish. "I use heavy line and work it real slowly so it almost hangs in the water. I recommend a blue shimmer skirt if the water is clear and a bright white skirt if the water is off-color."

If there is shallow grass in the lake, Scalish may go to a Shad Rap, ticking it just above the grass. When it hangs up on grass, he rips it free and prepares for the strike.

Now that you know the secrets of ice-out bassin', are you willing to put up with numb fingers to give it a try?

SPRING

The migration, mating rituals
and propagation of the species …

TARGET TRIBUTARIES where runoff from spring rains raises the water temperature and as a result, brings the bass into the shallows.

STRATEGIES FOR WARMING WATER
A step-by-step guide for locating bass in spring

SOMETIMES IT'S EASY TO FORGET that bass aren't pictures in a magazine, but living, breathing creatures, driven by their need for food, procreation and survival. Knowing where and how bass react to changes in their environment goes to the very heart of solving the bass fishing riddle.

As winter turns to spring and the water warms, bass exhibit marked, predictable movements. Two experts on the topic are BASS ace Ron Shuffield and Fish Fishburne, the charismatic host of the tournament trail weigh-ins and a former pro himself. The tournament résumés of both anglers are weighted heavy on the springtime side of the fishing game, and their wisdom should help you put more lunkers in your livewell during this exciting bass fishing season.

WHY WATER WARMS

Exactly why does the temperature of your local lake, river or pond increase in spring? Shuffield and Fishburne offer these reasons:

Increasing air temperature — "Obviously, when the air begins to warm, everything it touches warms, too, including the surface of our lakes and rivers," Shuffield notes. "The top layer of water warms first; deep water may remain cold for a much longer period of time."

Longer days — "As daylight increases with the arrival of spring, the amount of time the water is exposed to the warming rays of the sun increases," Fishburne says.

Seasonal rains — "Spring is a season of frequent and often heavy rainfall in many regions," Ron adds. "Warm rains can increase the temperature of a body of water very rapidly. Runoff from spring rains typically enters a reservoir system via the tributaries and headwaters; these areas will warm up quickly, perhaps overnight."

Muddy waters — "With heavy rainfall, the lake often turns muddy; when the weather clears, dark water absorbs the heat of the sun much more effectively than clear water," Fishburne says. "Therefore, murky lakes and rivers are typically the first to warm in spring, while clear bodies of water may take much longer to warm."

WARMING TREND

A welcomed warming trend in late winter/early spring always gets many Bassmasters out of their LA-Z-Boys and into their bass boats for the first fishing trip of the season.

"If there are two or three mild, sunny days in a row in late February or early March, and the water temp bumps up a degree or two — say from 42 to 44 degrees — bass often move a little shallower from their winter haunts," Shuffield points out. "They've been deep all winter, and they'll typically move up to the first breakline — often from 25 to 20 feet deep in a clear lake, 15 to 12 feet in a murky lake. Banks with a fairly fast taper are usually best in late winter, because a bass doesn't have to move but a few feet to change depths. If a fish were on a flat, it might have to swim 50 yards to move 3 feet shallower."

This initial breakline can be subtle and easily overlooked.

"During this first warm spell, fishermen always ask, 'Have the bass moved up yet?' " Fishburne adds. "But there's seldom a wholesale movement of bass this early in the year. Sometimes only a few fish may slide up shallow, but the good news is, they're often big. It's not unusual to have only one bite on a jig during a late February trip, but that fish will be a 6- to 9-pounder."

A patient approach is a must. "Late winter bass will be extremely sluggish; you'll usually have to fish very slowly to get bit," Shuffield warns. The favorite lure of both pros during this initial warmup — often the only lure

Hunt For Hot Water

■ **Type of lake** — River-run reservoir in the mid-South.

■ **Features** — Extensive flooded buckbrush, stumpfields and occasional patches of vegetation.

■ **Time of year** — Early spring.

■ **Best pattern** — Bass are moving from the main lake into large bays and secondary pockets, where they will spawn. Focus on banks and secondary points in the warmest creeks. A temperature gauge is essential for finding water that is warmer than other areas. Cast spinnerbaits to cover (laydowns, brush, etc.) along deeper banks, or run small crawfish crankbaits over gravel or rocky bottoms. Move from cove to cove and cover plenty of water.

■ **Key to success** — Try banks with direct exposure to the warming southern sun. These will be warmer than other banks.

Patterning Late Winter/Spring Bass
By The Numbers

Lake Temperature	General Bass Location	Best Fishing Approach
38-42 Degrees	Bass will be deep (20-35 feet) in clear lakes, shallower (10-15 feet) in murky lakes. Target points, channel drops and ledges. Bass in natural lakes may suspend near dropoffs in 7-10 feet of water.	Fish slowly with a 3/4-ounce jig-and-pig, making repeated casts to cover, or tight-line a leadhead grub or blade bait.
42-44 Degrees	Some bass will move up to the breakline and sit or suspend near cover. This initial movement is typically only a few feet shallower — if bass were at 30 feet, try 25.	Stay with the jig-and-pig or grub in the same spots. If bottom bumping doesn't pay off, try swimming the lure just off bottom.
44-48 Degrees	More bass will move to the first breakline. Around 46 degrees, a few big females may begin staging on objects along migration routes leading to shallow spawning areas.	Work a jig progressively shallower on steep points until you contact fish. Try jigs and suspending jerkbaits around isolated stumps and weed patches along ditches and creek channels accessing shallow bays.
48-55 Degrees	Bass are staging now on drops adjacent to spawning areas and isolated cover along migration routes. A few big bass may spawn around 55 degrees.	Use more active lures as water warms — big-bladed spinnerbaits and small crankbaits in murky water, suspending jerkbaits in clear lakes. Scan shallow bays for early spawners; use floating worms and tube baits on any you encounter.
55-60 Degrees	Many bass will be staging, and greater numbers will be moving in to spawn.	Try spinnerbaits and small crankbaits on drops and isolated cover for stagers; floating worms and tube baits for early bedders.
60-70 Degrees	Bass will be either moving in to spawn, spawning, or leaving the nest.	Target prespawners on migration routes and drops close to bedding areas with spinnerbaits and small crankbaits; catch spawners with floating worms and tube baits, and postspawners with topwaters and minnow imitators.
70-80 Degrees	A few bass will spawn from 70-75 degrees, but many have left the nest via migration routes to deeper, more open water.	Begin by targeting any remaining spawners with floating worms and Gitzits. Try surface lures and buzzbaits in 72-76 degree water in spawning perimeters. Gradually follow migration routes back to main lake with crankbaits and Carolina rigs.

they'll bother using — is a jig-and-pig.

"Fish it painfully slow across the bottom in deep water around wood and rock cover," Shuffield advises. "Winter bass feed mainly on crawfish, and a jig simulates a live craw to a T." In superclear lakes without much wood cover, Shuffield may try to tempt a sluggish bass with a leadhead grub fished on light line.

Often the first significant spring bite occurs when the lake warms from around 46 to 50 degrees. In some lakes, this can be the beginning of the "staging" period. "This term has been misused so much, it's led to a lot of confusion among bass anglers," Fishburne says. "I define staging as the period before the spawn when female bass hold in slightly deeper areas to fatten up. They're trying to get their body weight up because they won't be feeding for a while once they're on the beds." He looks for staging bass around targets such as laydown logs, boulders, stumps and (his favorite) boat docks.

Finding Springtime Bass

As water temperatures warm, bass patterns change. Use these guidelines from experts Ron Shuffield and Fish Fishburne in conjunction with a surface temperature meter to find and catch bass throughout the spring season.

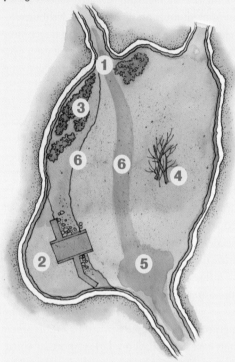

1 — Check warming water in tributaries for spring bass.
2 — Bass tend to follow rising water in early spring. A flooded launch ramp or parking lot has been known to hold bass.
3 — Warming water stimulates new weed growth, which will attract bass.
4 — In early spring, when bass are still deep, a swimming pool thermometer might be more useful than one that reads surface temperatures. Tie a line to it and use it to monitor deep structure.
5 — The few days following lake turnover in spring are typically tough. Try a finesse lure where the clear and murky water meet.
6 — Seek out the original river or creek banks when water levels are fluctuating.

"Deeper docks are great places to catch staging bass in tributaries," he says. "Use a worm or jig and keep it around the 7-foot zone — this is a magic depth now."

"The first bass to stage are often the biggest,"

Shuffield adds. "I'm convinced these superior bass are genetically programmed to get to the best spawning areas first. They're heavy with eggs, and there can be lots of them. In March tournaments, you'll see some huge bags of fish weighed in when the lake is bumping 50 degrees."

Shuffield looks for staging bass on key holding areas along "migration routes" — creek channels cutting along steep banks and points, ditches and contours leading from deep to shallow water. If there's a brushpile or a stump along these bass highways, you'll find fish. His favorite lures for staging bass include jigs, grubs and suspending jerkbaits, all fished slowly.

Staging activity is in full swing by the time the surface temperature hits 55 degrees. Both pros employ faster moving lures now — heavy spinnerbaits,

A JIG PITCHED to cover along key migration routes is Ron Shuffield's primary means of catching prespawn bass.

FISH FISHBURNE always has a tube jig ready for action should he pass a spawning bed while fishing down a shoreline.

small flat-sided crankbaits, jerkbaits twitched aggressively — but will revert to the jig if the bite is slow. "Bass will be stationed anywhere from the shoreline to the first dropoff," Shuffield reveals. "I've seen big largemouth already on their beds in this temperature range, so keep your eyes peeled for spawners."

The 55 to 60 degree range can be tricky. Bass may suspend off spawning flats now in 7 to 10 feet

USE A JIG-AND-PIG in deepwater structure during the first warming trend of the year. Pick a heavy size first for bottom hugging bass, then a lighter one to swim through those that are suspending.

of water; Shuffield recommends a lure capable of probing the middle band of water, such as a jerkbait or medium running crankbait. Fishburne prefers to ignore suspending fish and target more catchable bass near bottom cover; he'll use a wide wobbling crankbait, tube jig or Texas rigged worm.

BEDDING BASICS

Between 60 and 65 degrees, both pros expect bass to be transitioning into a shallow spawning pattern. "The best bedding places are sheltered coves, pockets or bays with isolated wood or weed patches, a hard bottom and relatively clear water," notes Fishburne, a proficient sight fisherman. Wearing polarized sunglasses, he visually scans these spots for signs of bedding fish or bass cruising up and down the banks; the latter are looking for a good place to nest.

"A floating worm is awesome right now," he emphasizes. "Most anglers use a bright color, but bass on pressured lakes can learn to avoid the bubblegum and hot orange worms. In a tournament, I often have better luck on darker, more subdued worms." The pro also keeps rods rigged with a tube bait and lizard during the bedding period, alternating casts with these lures until he eventually tempts a bedding fish into biting.

Bedding never occurs all at once, but rather in waves, Shuffield adds. "If you don't see bass on beds now, don't panic — they haven't moved up quite yet. In a spring tournament, when most other fishermen are sight fishing, I'll often target prespawn bass instead; they're far more aggressive than bedding fish. Comb the perimeter of potential bedding areas with a small crankbait, like a Shad Rap, for prespawners."

POSTSPAWN SAVVY

Many bass will be finished spawning once the water tops 70 degrees. Fishburne continues to target bedding areas, gradually working his way back out to deeper water via ditches and channels as the lake warms. "Prespawn bass can be moody — some may smash your lure while others just follow or roll lazily on it. A floating worm and a small minnow imitator are my favorites now."

Shuffield prefers topwater baits for active postspawn bass, especially the Heddon Zara Spook and Storm Chug Bug; he fishes these close to bedding areas. If a topwater bite doesn't materialize, he'll move to nearby grasslines and break out his confidence lure, a jig-and-pig. "I'll start by swimming a 1/2-ounce jig along the inside edges of grasslines, then as the water warms, I'll flip a 3/4-ounce jig into the deeper outside edges."

All of these patterns generally hold up until the water reaches 80 degrees. Then our pros work the shallows at first light, and move to offshore points and channel drops as bass get into their summer routine. "Late winter through spring is definitely the best time for a lunker bass, and arguably the most exciting weeks of the year to be on the water," Fishburne declares.

More Tips For Warming Water

■ Avoid current and cold, muddy water on your first bass fishing outings in late winter/early spring.

■ Early spring rains can facilitate a wholesale movement of forage and bass. Warm rains entering via the tributaries can warm the system quickly and cause hibernating crawfish to hatch; try small craw-imitating jigs and crankbaits in the back ends of tributaries, where the water is often 5 degrees warmer than elsewhere after a hard rain.

■ Bass tend to follow rising water in early spring. Some Bassmasters report catching bass in flooded launch ramp parking lots following a sudden rise caused by heavy rainfall.

■ Always look for the first weed growth in early spring. You'll usually find it in the northwest section of the lake.

■ In early spring, when bass are still deep, a swimming pool thermometer may be more useful than a surface temperature gauge. Tie a line to it and use it to monitor the temperature on deep structures.

■ The few days following lake turnover in spring are typically tough. Look for areas where clear and murky water meet, then try a small lure — like a leadhead grub.

■ Many reservoirs undergo a forage shift from crawfish to shad as the water warms and plankton blooms develop. As the shad bite becomes more dominant, switch to lures with some flash, like spinnerbaits, small crankbaits and jerkbaits.

■ In reservoirs with a fluctuating water level, look for the original river or creek banks — bass often hold here in large numbers.

A GOOD WAY TO FIND postspawn bass is by backtracking along the same migration routes the fish used to reach the shallows.

DAVID FRITTS **says a hard lake bottom attracts prespawn bass most of the time.**

STAGING AREAS: KEYS TO SPRING SUCCESS

Find the bass' stopover spots between winter and spring locations

TWO WORDS DESCRIBE PRESPAWN fishing action: feast and famine. If you've spent much time looking for bass during those fabulous — yet sometimes bewildering — days of spring, you know what that means. One day you catch 'em like crazy — and big ones — and the next day you'd swear the bass had packed up and left the state.

They haven't. In fact, the pros say prespawn bass are among the easiest fish to catch and pattern, once you learn to identify the types of areas they use prior to the spawn. The fish are schooled up, feed often and will hit a wide variety of lures. But because they are schooled in small areas, finding them requires a little work and patience.

Those areas, commonly called "staging areas," are structure-specific spots on the lake that bass use as safe havens before they move onto the beds. Those hot spots are located somewhere between the spawning flats and their deeper wintering areas.

Unfortunately, many anglers believe that the spawning area provides the best fishing. While bedding areas are easier to find and may produce very big bass, catching that bass can test your nerves. It may take an hour or more to convince a bass to strike. Conversely, staging bass are more predictable and willing to strike, says four time Bassmaster Classic champion Rick Clunn.

"I don't enjoy fishing for bedding bass," he says.

(Opposite page) BECAUSE OF **their aggressive nature, staging bass are more reliable than spawning fish, according to Rick Clunn.**

"I prefer to chase prespawn bass around the lake. On larger lakes, it's common to find bass in different phases of the seasonal pattern. So, I target the section of the lake that's most likely in

Best Bet For Big Bass

■ **Type of lake** — Western water storage reservoir.
■ **Features** — Small canyon impoundment known for huge bass.
■ **Time of year** — Early spring.
■ **Best pattern** — With the water temperature edging toward the magic mid-60s range, big bass are staging on main lake humps, ridges and points just out from shallow spawning coves. These fish are concentrated, and they are aggressive in their feeding habits. Work structure in the 12- to 18-foot-depth range with 3/8-ounce football-head hair jigs tipped with pork frogs or scented worms.
■ **Key to success** — Select structures carefully according to location, depth and cover elements, then work them with extreme thoroughness and patience to trigger strikes from big bass.

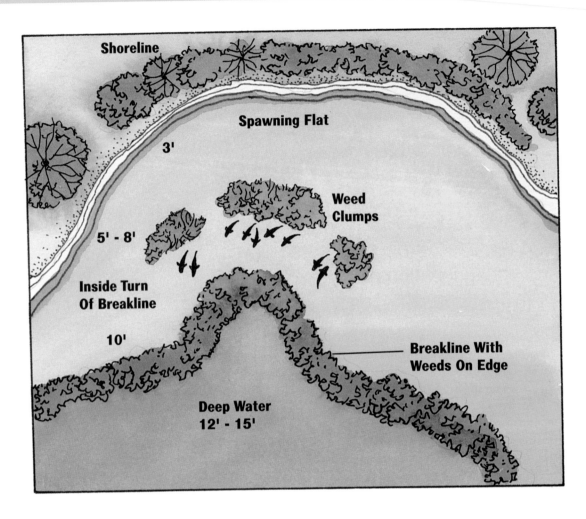

BASS CONGREGATE around inside turns along the nearest dropoff before scattering onto spawning flats. A combination with a hard bottom and scattered weeds is a prime area.

Shoreline

Spawning Flat

3'

Weed Clumps

5' - 8'

Inside Turn Of Breakline

10'

Breakline With Weeds On Edge

Deep Water 12' - 15'

the prespawn pattern at that time of the year."

Water temperature dictates spring bass movement, both to and from the spawning flats. As a rule, the north side of the lake warms up first because of the angle of the sun that time of year and protection from cooler, northwesterly winds. On most reservoirs, the shallower upper end of the lake will warm up faster than the lower end, so it's likely you can find prespawn bass at various stages throughout the spring.

As the water warms, fish move out of deeper holes toward the shallows. Depending upon the region of the country, the migration can begin when water temperatures are in the high 40s in northern lakes to the mid-50s on southern waters.

"There are no hard, fast rules for when bass

move from winter to prespawn patterns," says Indiana pro Chip Harrison. "Although we're told bass don't nest until water temperatures reach the mid-60s, I've seen northern bass on beds in the mid-50s. Our prespawn action begins the day after the ice leaves the lakes."

Just as warming trends lure fish to the shallows, cold fronts that chill the water will drive them back. If you know where bass stage during the prespawn, you stand a good chance of relocating them when weather pushes them away from spawning grounds.

Veteran North Carolina pro Guy Eaker Sr. knows that as well as anyone. His experience with moody prespawn bass played a major role in a BASS victory on Sam Rayburn Lake, the sprawling

East Texas fishery renowned for producing huge catches of staging bass.

Like most anglers, Eaker began catching bass in shallow bushes during practice for the February tournament, but he knew the pattern wouldn't hold up.

"There were some fronts forecast for the rest of the week, so I figured those fish would back off," he recalls. "I abandoned the shoreline pattern and spent the rest of the practice looking for staging areas adjacent to spawning flats. I found eight of them, and that was the key to my winning."

He finished the tournament with 15 bass weighing 49 pounds, more than a 3-pound average per fish.

Staging areas differ from lake to lake and in various regions around the country. At Rayburn the key areas were depressions on large flats.

"I idled out of the creek channel onto a 3- to 4-foot flat," he describes. "I'd drive around until I found a depression that maybe only dropped to a foot or two deeper. That's where those fish were holding."

Staging areas usually provide the bass a deeper sanctuary than they have on spawning grounds. Those transition areas can be along the main river channel, which may offer the deepest water in the lake, or as shallow as those slight depressions Eaker found on Rayburn.

"The depth at which they stage often depends upon the part of country you're fishing, the overall depth of the lake, and how far along the lake is in the prespawn season," adds BASS pro David Fritts. "In Florida, where there isn't a lot of deep water, the staging area will be a lot shallower than what you may find in big reservoirs with deep water."

In other words, there is no magical depth anglers should target when searching for staging areas. Also, it's important to note that staging areas can change during the prespawn season. Locations that bass use during the early prespawn will likely be deeper than those they use as the spawn draws nearer.

As the prespawn season progresses, bass will move to the inside edge of a breakline, especially if cover is present, before heading onto the spawning flat. But don't concentrate all your efforts in one spot. The fish don't all spawn together, so pros like Fritts are conscious that even though fish have left the breakline others are likely moving up behind them to take their place.

During stable weather, Fritts believes those fish can make a sudden move shallower, even though

DAVID FRITTS remains conscious that even though fish have committed to a spawning area, others will likely take their place on the same breakline vacated by their predecessors.

PRESPAWN BASS in reservoirs hold in deeper water adjacent to spawning grounds. However, the depth variance between staging and spawning areas is very subtle.

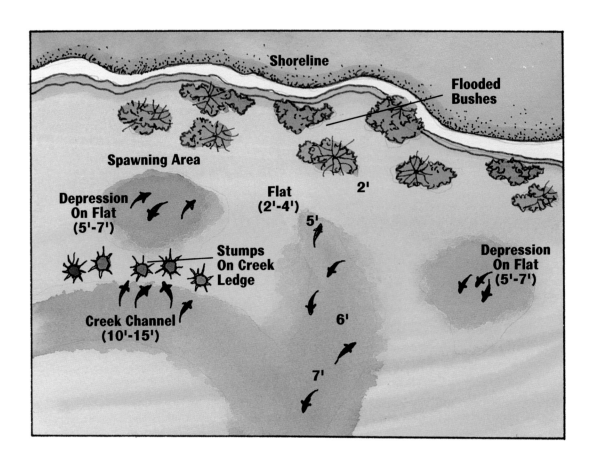

Shoreline

Flooded Bushes

Spawning Area

Depression On Flat (5'-7')

Flat (2'-4')

2'

5'

Stumps On Creek Ledge

Depression On Flat (5'-7')

6'

Creek Channel (10'-15')

7'

it's not very far from a deeper staging area. That's what happened to Fritts and Arkansas pro Mark Davis during a BASS tournament held on Alabama's Lake Eufaula during March. Fritts finished third and Davis 10th, but had the weather turned sour, the results could well have been different.

"We were fishing for prespawn fish in the same main lake cove, except Mark was working the creek ledge while I was concentrating on ditches that ran out of the creek onto the spawning flats," Fritts describes. "We were only a cast or two apart."

Davis led the first day of the tournament with a five bass catch that weighed nearly 30 pounds, but only caught three more fish over the next two days. Fritts' action, meanwhile, got better each day.

"My area proved to be a better one because the weather stayed so good," Fritts recalls. "After the first day, the fish weren't stopping to feed along the

creek channel Mark was fishing — they were moving right up into the ditches leading onto the flat. Had a front come through, Mark's pattern would have been a lot stronger."

Fritts agrees that staging areas don't have to be significantly deeper than spawning grounds to congregate bass following a weather change, yet he's seen situations in which the bass moved a long distance to deep water after a front had passed.

"Each lake has its own quirky characteristics," he explains. "You just have to check several areas and learn to rely upon past experiences."

Also, cover is a key ingredient, but not always. He's found bass to simply back off to a sandy or hard bottom with no cover around.

"I believe a hard bottom is a major attraction for prespawn bass 99 percent of the time," Fritts insists. "If there's grass there, look for the openings in the grass that may indicate a harder bottom. That's where the fish will be."

Harrison says that holds true in northern natural lakes, where early season bass use inside turns on weed edges of breaklines more than they use the points for migration.

"I don't think they ever leave the inside edge during the spring," he says. "On our lakes, the fish don't go much deeper than 12 feet during that prespawn period, regardless of what the weather does. The key is to find the subtle inside turns that have weeds growing along the outer edge, and sand on the inside edge."

Again, it's important to note that not all prespawn movement occurs at once or during the heart of early spring. In fact, some large females will move extremely shallow while most of the lake's bass are schooling in deeper staging areas.

For example, Oklahoma pro Tommy Biffle believes there's an early migration long before most anglers realize it. He says he catches bass very shallow in later winter by targeting areas where a creek channel bends into a bank covered with scattered rock and bushes.

"Many of the really big bass migrate into shallow water before settling back into the traditional staging areas," he describes. "It can happen as early as January or February, providing that several warm, sunny days have warmed the water enough to pull the females into the shoreline bushes.

"I think they're there to absorb the warmth more than they are to spawn. You can really catch a big stringer by flipping jigs during the warmer days, but a cold snap will push them out."

Northern bass have similar habits. Within a few days after ice leaves a lake, Mishawaka, Ind., angler Al Gearhart finds big bass lying on muck bottoms in 2 feet of water or less in wind-protected coves. The dark bottom absorbs the heat from the sun, and he believes the females are using that warmth to ripen the eggs they are carrying.

"I find them lying flat on the bottom in areas where you won't see them spawning later," he describes. "They're not as aggressive as most pre-

DURING PRESPAWN
David Fritts uses fast-moving crankbaits during stable weather and a jig following a frontal passage.

spawn bass, but they will bite if you get a jig or live bait on their noses."

When bass bunch up later in the prespawn, they're receptive to a variety of lures. Especially fast movers, such as crankbaits, spinnerbaits and jerkbaits. During weather fronts, slower presentations, such as jigs, may be required.

"The jig and the crankbait are two of your most reliable lures that time of year," says Fritts. "They best resemble crawfish, which I think the bass are feeding on mostly.

"Crankbaits, I believe, will trigger that impulsive strike that can get the entire school active. Once you get them going, you can really catch a mess of big fish."

SPRINGTIME BASS
like to congregate in depressions near shallow water. Bottom-bounce or swim a jig through these deeper areas to con them into biting.

PREDICTING LUNKER DAYS
Hunting for a spring trophy?
It pays to know when to go

TOO MANY DAYS to fish and not enough time to go. That is the perplexing challenge bass anglers face in springtime, the prime season for catching lunkers. Some days are better than others for catching a lunker, meaning that timing is everything.

To determine which days during this brief window of opportunity are best for landing a trophy requires access to a weather forecast and a few facts about bass and their environment.

**(Opposite page)
SPRINGTIME AND top-
waters go hand-in-
hand. Keep one tied
on long enough, and
a trophy bass could
be your reward.**

THE PERFECT SCENARIO

After a winter of little or no feeding, bass are anxious to restore lost muscle and fat reserve as they prepare for the rigors of spawning. Their body mass may not yet be optimal, but most females should be heavy with roe, which, according to fisheries scientists, can add as much as 10 percent to their weight.

Being cold-blooded, a bass' metabolism depends not only on the temperature of its surroundings, but also on what direction the mercury is going. Cooling water can slam the door on the fish's feeding mood, stable temperatures maintain the status quo, and warming water is like three chocolate bars washed down with five cups of coffee.

Believe it or not, an optimum scenario for catching lunkers occurs when surface temperatures reach the high 40s. There is very little to eat, so the predators are particularly vulnerable to lures. Generally, the water has to warm into the 50s before salamanders, frogs and other edibles slither out of hibernation and make themselves available for dinner.

The high 40s also suggests the bigger bass will

March Moon Madness

■ **Type of lake** — Lowland reservoir in the East.
■ **Features** — Average depth is less than 10 feet; grassbeds and cypress stumps are the two main types of cover.
■ **Time of year** — Spring.
■ **Best pattern** — Trophy bass will be in the prespawn phase until just before the full moon in March and they will be feeding aggressively. Fish spinnerbaits, jig-and-pigs and lipless crankbaits around shallow stump flats and other staging areas prior to the spawn. When bass begin bedding, fish Texas rigged worms or twitch baits over shallow, sandy bottoms, especially where beds are spotted.
■ **Key to success** — Keep moving and working areas protected from the northeast wind to find pockets of prespawn and spawning bass.

THE BEST odds of landing a lunker are during the days leading up to the full moon.

still be dominating the food shelf. A number of studies by biologists verify that large bass are the first to move into the shallows in spring, with the smaller ones submissively waiting until approximately the 50 degree mark. This means your lure doesn't always have to fight its way through the 12-inchers to make it to the big boys.

The odds increase even more with the passage of a frontal system and even more so when it coincides with a full moon.

Springtime. Fourth day of warming water. High 40s. Front coming through. Full moon. These are the days to call in sick and chase lunkers.

AFTER THE TURNOVER

If your water ices up in the winter or at least comes close, it will usually experience that strange kind of thermal stratification under which the warmest layer (approximately 39 degrees, the temperature at which water is the heaviest) is found at the bottom and the coldest (approximately 32 degrees) is at the top. Most fish, therefore, hang around the bottom throughout winter, in various states of dormancy.

Sometime in the early spring, a good wind will come up and cause that body of water to turn over. The upper layers mix with the lower layers, and the water quickly becomes one uniform temperature, probably about 36 degrees. This means lunker bass, which had previously been snoozing in 39 degree water for a number of months, suddenly find themselves in colder water with current. While ini-

tially a turnoff and not a good time to go fishing, it will serve as a wakeup call for the bass and start a countdown for when you should get out there.

A little trick is to watch for that brown crud suddenly floating on the surface, a result of the new currents kicking up that decayed biomass that has been settling on the bottom since late last fall. Once you see it, pay particular attention to the weather forecast. You don't need an extreme warming trend; a mild one will do. Anglers and biologists alike have found that bass will seek out the warmest water available in spring, and that means the shallows in sun-baked coves or pockets, usually on the northern shores. Give these areas a day or two to warm up, and then fish them from about noon through the heat of the day.

SPRING'S FIRST WARMING

Possibly the best date on the lunker calendar for Northern and Southern folks alike is that first elongated spell of relatively great weather. Here, the key word is *relative*, as in ratio of air temperature to water temperature. If your water hovered in the mid-50s all winter, you're going to need a few 70 degree days to fire up the big ones. If it was more like 38 degree water, a spell of 55 degree days may be all you need.

Wherever and whenever it occurs, a warm day with sunshine and a stiff breeze can warm a small body of water a few degrees from top to bottom (larger and deeper lakes take longer). If there is little or no wind, yet plenty of sun, the upper few feet can gain as much as 5 to 8 degrees in one afternoon (some of that, however, may be lost again during the night). So, even though the first day of a warm spell has potential, things just keep getting better and better the longer you wait. The only thing you have to worry about is another angler beating you to the punch.

ENSUING WARM SPELLS

That first major warm front is usually the best for lunkers, but each one thereafter is also worth playing hooky for, with perhaps some slight

The Making of Spring's Post-Turnover Lunker Day

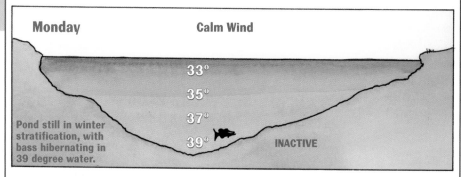

Monday   **Calm Wind**

33°
35°
37°
39°   INACTIVE

Pond still in winter stratification, with bass hibernating in 39 degree water.

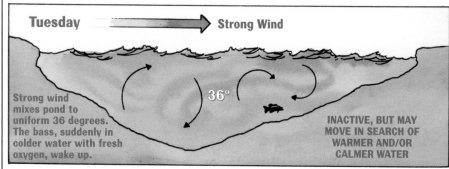

Tuesday ➝ **Strong Wind**

36°

Strong wind mixes pond to uniform 36 degrees. The bass, suddenly in colder water with fresh oxygen, wake up.

INACTIVE, BUT MAY MOVE IN SEARCH OF WARMER AND/OR CALMER WATER

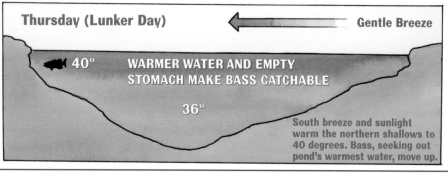

Thursday (Lunker Day) ⬅ Gentle Breeze

40°   WARMER WATER AND EMPTY STOMACH MAKE BASS CATCHABLE

36°

South breeze and sunlight warm the northern shallows to 40 degrees. Bass, seeking out pond's warmest water, move up.

---

adjustments along the way. For example, as the water temperature gets closer to the 60s, you may not need a sunny day quite so much. In fact, a cloudy day toward the end of a warm spell can provide some excellent action in the shallows, assuming you can contend with catching all those smaller bass along with the big ones. You may also start seeing some big bass action at dawn and dusk, besides that heat-of-the-day period.

THE SPAWNING MOON

Once your water reaches into the 60s, the weather begins to stabilize and the bass fishing generally gets good, making those warm weather lunker days less distinctive. But with feeding a top priority for the approaching spawn, there may be a three to four day period that month you won't want to miss. It starts four days prior to the full moon and runs right up to the day it is full.

Underwater observations have shown that a bass' spawning cycle can be related to the lunar phase and especially during a full moon. The bass bite well during this period, and if the weather is good, they hit very well. If the weather is bad, they hold off until next month's full moon, and the action is even more fantastic.

Furthermore, it has long been reported by many experienced anglers that just prior to laying their eggs, the females often school in a holding area fairly near the spawning grounds, such as a relatively steep point or bluff adjacent to a protected cove with a firm substrate. If you can find this school, you can load up on a year's worth of lunkers in just a few hours.

THE LUNAR PHASE

By late spring, the weather has stabilized, the water is stratified and, with food everywhere, the bass fishing is as about as good as it gets, slowly tapering off into the summer months. About the only variable left is the moon, particularly those few days before and after each new and full moon, plus the half moon. In clear water, your bass may feed at night under the light of the full moon, so either go then or concentrate more on the other two phases. In murky water, there shouldn't be much difference in respect to light, but there can be in terms of electromagnetic energy.

TOPWATER BAITS may not bring as many bites as other lures in the spring, but the ones that hit will most likely be of better quality.

SUMMER

Make the most of bass fishing
during the longest days of the year ...

A SPINNERBAIT is a good option for hungry postspawn bas.

TEXTBOOK PATTERNS FOR THE POSTSPAWN PERIOD

Look for bass in these hot spots after the spawn

WHEN DAVID WHARTON WON a major BASS title on South Carolina's Lake Murray, he confided that his game plan in the mid-May competition involved following a "textbook postspawn pattern." The veteran Texas pro, who holds an education degree, can be forgiven if he sometimes talks like a schoolteacher.

But the point remains . . . do patterns exist that we can refer to and then implement the same way a scholar can index a subject and then find information on it?

"I believe so," says Wharton. "For example, on lakes such as Murray and Sam Rayburn, which have both aquatic vegetation and fluctuating water levels, one well-defined area in particular tends to attract bass year after year when reproduction ends."

GRASSLINES

Wharton suggests that the best textbook locale on impoundments such as these possesses several characteristics: First, a distinct, shallow grassline or edge grows on a point that runs from shallow to deep water. In effect, this vegetation serves as the first good form of cover between shallow and deep water.

Furthermore, he zeros in on where the grass forms a point. Typically, that grassy point will lie in water at least several feet deeper than most of the weedlines.

Wharton says this occurs because on impoundments where the water rises and falls, grass that remains submerged grows faster and more lush than that which is periodically exposed to the air. Again, this break is very noticeable and easy to find on a depthfinder.

Now this type of locale is certainly a good one, instructs Wharton, but it becomes a "textbook" spot if it exists near docks and/or buckbrush in the backs of pockets. For instance, at the Lake Murray event he probed similar pockets early in the morning, where the fish had temporarily moved shallow. The rest of the day, both Wharton and the bass spent their time on those grassy points.

Regarding lures, Wharton likes baits that will run across the top of the submerged grass. At Murray, he employed a 3/4-ounce Stanley spinnerbait

with No. 3 and 4 willowleaf blades. Willowleaf blades are always the choice for salad because they slip through better than other configurations. He also likes to slow roll the spinnerbait so that it barely ticks the top of the cover.

Likewise, lipless crankbaits are preferred over other cranks because anglers can regulate the lure's depth easier. The rod tip can be used to control the depth of the lipless crankbait, which tends to remain at the same level and doesn't "pop up" like a flat crankbait, Wharton notes.

He typically opts for a Luhr Jensen Sugar Shad in chrome blue, crawfish red or patterns with orange in them.

Finally, for the grass, Wharton will tie on a Texas rigged plastic worm that has had its sinker pegged so that weeds will not separate the bait from the sinker. The nine time Classic qualifier slowly slithers the crawler through the cover.

And for that brief period when the bass feed on the surface before moving deep, Wharton works a Luhr Jensen P-J Pop around the docks and buckbrush.

Postspawn Stopovers

■ **Type of lake** — Large, mainstream reservoir in the South.

■ **Features** — Classic structure lake with extensive flats — divided by stump lined creek and river channels.

■ **Time of year** — Late spring/early summer.

■ **Best pattern** — After bass have finished spawning, their first stops on their way back to deep water will be along shallow ditches and drops adjacent to the spawning flats, typically in 5 to 6 feet of water. The fish concentrate around stumps, logs and other cover objects along these submerged migration routes. Find these secondary channels by cross-referencing topo maps and depthfinder returns. Fish them with crankbaits, spinnerbaits and finesse worms.

■ **Key to success** — Finding cover on the edges of these shallow dropoffs is essential. The more cover a drop has, the larger the school of bass it's likely to hold.

CHANNEL LEDGES

Perennial Bassmaster Classic qualifier and former BASS points champion Gary Klein becomes extremely enthusiastic on the topic of textbook postspawn patterns.

"The postspawn period is one of those times of the year when the fishing can be absolutely phenomenal," says Klein, another Texas pro with two decades of experience on the tournament trail. "Some 80 percent of a lake's population of big female bass has been on the banks to spawn.

"Whereas those big females have been scattered all over a lake's shorelines, when they move off the banks and begin their move to deep water the bass regroup en masse at just a few well-defined places."

Klein instructs that lips of creek and river channels are prime sanctuaries for those largemouth and that 30- to 40-pound stringers are possible there. The key, of course, is to break down the topography of a lake and concentrate on very specific lips or channel edges. He does this by beginning his search on the upper one-third of a body of water.

"In the upper sections of a lake, fishermen will find it easier to see where fish have been and where they are likely to go," Klein educates. "Even a large impoundment becomes very small when you start to break it down into thirds and then narrow your search even further.

"Once I am on the upper third of a lake, I search for spawning flats that lead to the lips or edges of a channel. Then I look for water depths between 8 and 20 feet along the channel. Finally, I tune in to breaklines along the channel at those depths."

Klein notes that he may have to check out several of those breaklines before he finds a huge concentration of bass. But those bass can be tracked down through diligence, and once an angler does so, another textbook postspawn pattern kicks in.

To fully exploit that pattern, Klein systematically employs a series of lures. First, he cranks the channel edge with deep running baits, such as the Norman DD 22, Poe's 300 and 400 series and Mann's Plus models. He switches back and forth among these baits, constantly trying to give the bass different looks.

But these "crankplugs," as Klein calls them, are not his main choice. After he has caught a few largemouth, he switches to a Carolina rig and methodically mines the entire breakline on the channel edge. (The essentials of this rig include 20-pound-test Trilene Big Game for the main line, a 1-ounce egg sinker, 14-pound-test Trilene XT for the leader, and 6-inch Berkley Power Lizards in rootbeer or pumpkin-pepper with chartreuse tails.)

Klein says it is not unusual for him to catch a bass on each of the crankbaits and then round out a limit and begin the culling process with the Carolina rig.

And the pro still is not finished deciphering this textbook postspawn locale.

"Again, I want to emphasize I am thinking 'groups' of bass instead of individual fish on a textbook channel edge," he teaches. "For example, early in the morning, people usually will position their boats in deep water and throw toward the shallows when they work a breakline. A strike usually occurs after the plug has dug along the bottom then breaks free when it comes to the channel lip.

"But after the morning bite concludes, the bass reposition and sink deeper. Then I move the boat into the shallows and throw deep, which enables me to maintain contact with the bottom better. Finally, I'll reposition the boat once more so that it is parallel to the channel, and then maybe I can catch still more fish."

AS THE BASS MIGRATE from the shallow spawning flats to deeper water, anglers can pick them off by keying on migration routes, using a Carolina rigged lizard.

SECONDARY POINTS

Texas pro Bruce Benedict declares that secondary points in coves form the basis for a third textbook postspawn pattern — one that rings true on both flatland impoundments and highland reservoirs.

"After the fish finish their spawning ritual, they use creeks that run from coves as their migration paths to deep water," Benedict instructs. "At the same time, baitfish will migrate along those creek channels because they, like the bass, are heading for deep water to spend the summer.

"What you should look for are secondary points that make contact with or come near creek channels. But for those points to become 'textbook spots,' they must either have wood or rock cover on them, and they must also create some kind of breakline."

Benedict explains that bass use that cover to ambush the passing shad. On flatland impoundments, the cover typically takes the form of standing trees, submerged brush or stumps. On highland reservoirs, look for rockpiles or small boulders.

He says that water clarity is the single most important factor on how deep the bass hold. On clear upland impoundments, he has observed bass positioned where the bottom plunges from 20 to 50 feet. On stained lowland lakes, bass are more likely to position at places where the bottom drops from 5 to 15 feet.

Regarding lures, Benedict sometimes tries Zara Spooks or Smithwick Rattlin' Rogues to exploit the topwater bite. But his No. 1 surface artificial is a real surprise.

"I really rely on a 97 MR MirrOlure, a thin, 4 1/2-inch plug that is a saltwater bait," he confides. "The reason this lure is so effective, I believe, is that it holds an extremely loud knocker inside.

"I stumbled on to this bait one time while fish-

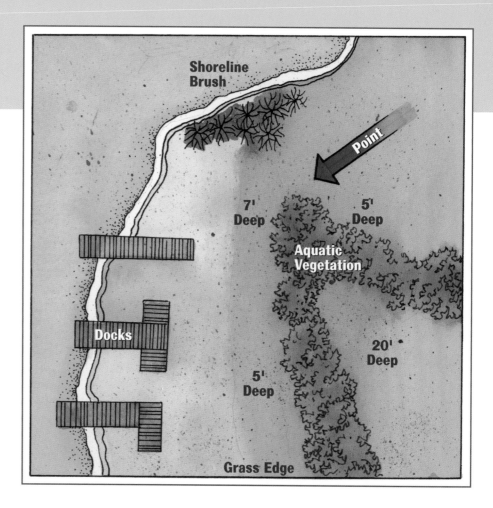

ing for redfish off the Texas coast. It eventually occurred to me that if it caught saltwater fish, maybe it would work for bass. Anyway, I used the Mirr-Olure to take about half my fish in a fourth place finish at the Bassmaster 25th Anniversary tournament at Beaver Lake in 1992."

Benedict retrieves the floating lure with this cadence: twitch, twitch, pause; twitch, pause; repeat. He allows the bait to rise to within 3 to 4 inches of the surface before he jerks it down once again. Strikes almost always occur on the rise.

Furthermore, an angler should hold his rod tip above his head when he initially casts this saltwater bait. As the lure nears him, he should gradually move his arms downward until the end of the cast, when his arms and the rod tip are pointed straight down.

Professors Wharton, Klein and Benedict may not be tenured university instructors, but they hold advanced doctorate degrees when it comes to bass behavior. It may even be said that they wrote the book (or at least three chapters) on textbook postspawn patterns.

IN WEEDY lakes that fluctuate in level, a band of sparse weed growth often exists between the shore and deeper, thicker weedbeds. In the postspawn, look for bass around shoreline cover early, and on grassy points by mid-morning.

FAKE BAITFISH rank at the top of the list for catching schooling bass.

SCHOOL'S OUT
Schooling bass are both fun and challenging to chase

T HERE IS NOTHING EASY about schooling fish. Just as the sirens of Greek mythology lured unsuspecting mariners to dangerous reefs, school bass sing a song that is every bit as sweet to the ears of fishermen. They tease. They taunt. They offer the seductive lyrics of splashing, feeding *visible* bass.

You know where they are and you know they are aggressive. According to commonly espoused bass fishing tenets, those are the two key ingredients to success. Unfortunately, school bass factor a gigantic dose of unpredictability into this equation, so much so that top professionals like Shaw Grigsby and Mike Folkestad seem to work harder at ignoring them than they do trying to catch them.

This dichotomy of thought is perhaps best expressed by Grigsby, a gold medal winner at the ESPN Great Outdoor Games. "In 20 years of competition, I cannot recall an event where I totally committed to schooling fish," he says. "Yet, there have been many days when I weighed in schooling fish."

Although cryptic in content, Grigsby simply expresses the delicate line any fisherman — tournament or recreational — must walk between capitalizing on the school frenzy and avoiding one of the greatest time wasters known to the angling art. The trick is knowing as much about *how* to catch them as *when* to catch them.

THE MIND-SET

Unless there are some rather unusual circumstances, schooling bass are not very big. Year in and year out, according to Grigsby, "The average schooling fish is going to be 2 pounds, it will be either a largemouth or a spotted bass, and it will be feeding on shad less than 2 inches long."

(Opposite page) CHOOSING A casting outfit and lure that can sail across a long distance to reach the fish is essential for school bass success.

Prime Spots For Schooling

■ **Type of lake** — Large natural lake in Florida.
■ **Features** — Abundant emergent weeds in shallower areas and hydrilla beds in deeper water.
■ **Time of year** — Late summer/early fall.
■ **Best pattern** — As summer wanes, pods of bass ranging from 1 1/2 to 4 pounds feed on shad in main lake areas. Best spots are wherever there is current: inflows and outflows into/from the lake, neckdowns between islands and outside grasslines. Keep moving and looking for baitfish or splashes where bass are feeding on schools of shad. Work these areas with shad-pattern Rat-L-Traps (1/2- or 1/4-ounce, matched to the baitfish size), soft jerkbaits or topwater lures.
■ **Key to success** — Schooling can occur at any time, but during a full moon, most action occurs at dawn and dusk.

SHAW GRIGSBY feels that fall offers the best odds for tying in to schooling bass.

Of course, Grigsby is the first to admit that fortunes have turned on the tug of a 2-pounder and that many a bass fisherman has ached for a limit of so-called "keeper" fish.

Just don't be fooled into thinking that school bass will supply something greater than a very average-size limit. In most cases, you will not upgrade much from fish to fish. And, if the pursuit of the schoolies takes up too much of the day, a fisherman could easily be missing out on the one or two strikes that will produce a truly memorable catch.

However, in keeping with the school bass' penchant for unpredictability, there are moments when the lights are on and everyone is home. And, everyone is big.

"I've seen them come up in places like West Point Lake on the Georgia-Alabama border," recalls Grigsby, "where they were all 9- and 10-pounders. And, I've seen cruising wolf packs that have been 4- and 5-pounders. It happens, but it is definitely not the norm."

One rare place where you can throw out any reasonable context of normality is in the legendary waters of Southern California's Lake Castaic, a place where weekly trout plants have altered the feeding habits of huge bass and turned them into equally enormous schooling fish.

Top western pro Mike Folkestad knows well what Castaic can offer, and he proves it regularly in his nontournament hours with limits that stagger even the most vivid imaginations. Just last winter, Mike and his son, Troy, combined for two limits (10 fish total) that weighed an amazing 75 pounds, 9 ounces. This doesn't even begin to consider their "off" days, when Mike nails a 14-4 or Troy nabs three for over 40 pounds.

THE SITUATION

By the time summer rolls around, the shad have spawned and multiplied. Plus, it is the time of year, says Folkestad, when most fishermen perceive schools as "fishable" and begin to make contact with them. Although schools of bass may exist year-round, this is the first time when most make a noticeable appearance.

Since shad are plankton feeders, they are guided by the rise and fall of their forage base, which tends to be geared to the sun.

As Grigsby has observed, "On overcast, cooler days, the shad don't come up as much, so you tend to look for warm, sunshiny days when the shad are up and active."

While this is a key to predicting where and when the shad will appear, it is but one of several factors that affect your guesswork. Another is wind (or current). Not only can wind action cause the baitfish to move around, it can alternately turn on or off their activity switch by its intensity.

These same elements apply in the other school-bass seasons during the fall and winter months. Of these two, Grigsby feels that fall offers the best opportunities, even better than summer, for more *dependable* schooling action. Dependable, of course, is a term to be defined loosely when referring to schooling bass — little is reliable about them.

The subject of dependability may be more apropos of man-made reservoirs, notes Grigsby, who believes that the lack of shoreline cover forces bass in these impoundments to be less bank-oriented and conditions them to a more open water feeding style.

To Folkestad, a western angler conditioned to fishing reservoirs devoid of shoreline cover, the winter months offer one of the best "contact times" for bass schooling in deep water. When asked if he meant "late fall" rather than "winter," Folkestad responded, "I mean it can be the dead of winter." (Don't forget, however, that Folkestad is referring to conditions in Southern California. Don't expect schooling action like that to occur often in northern latitudes.)

At such times, Folkestad finds schoolies by following main river channels or underwater points topping at 35 feet (with a rockpile, tree or bait school positioned on top) and breaking off into 50 or 60 feet of water. "They're gorging themselves on bait," counsels Folkestad, "and when you catch them, they're spitting up shad."

THE STRATEGY

For Grigsby and Folkestad, schooling bass are unquestionably a target of opportunity that can quickly relieve the pressure of boating a limit and open the rest of the day to the possibilities of finding that one, all-important kicker fish. Unfortunately, the consistency with which shad appear in any given area is almost nonexistent.

"Most of the time, it is very sporadic," observes Grigsby. "It is rare that you find bait in coves or pockets for weeks on end, usually it is a matter of days."

It is precisely for this reason that veteran anglers learn to ignore the schools, go about whatever other pattern they have discovered and remain alert for schooling fish that emerge within striking distance.

To make the most of this bonus potential, the onus is on choosing a lure and casting outfit that can sail across a long distance to reach the fish. Leading this casting hit parade is the venerable Zara Spook, a cigar-shaped stickbait that has gained legendary credentials not only for its casting performance, but for its ability to elicit strikes under a variety of conditions.

Other top choices include the renown Rebel Pop-R and Heddon Torpedo — smaller lures that do not measure up to the Spook in terms of distance, but can serve an angler well if the wind is favorable or the bass are working close.

The next glitch in this problematic assault on schooling bass is making the decision whether or not to chase the school. If it's a non-tournament situation, the decision becomes much easier, but the result may be just as frustrating. While a clear division often exists between tournament strategy and a fun-fishing attitude, it doesn't apply to

school bass. This is definitely a situation where cold, emotionless decision-making can make or break your day, whether or not a paycheck is on the line.

Should you chase them? Grigsby and Folkestad say yes. But only if you can get on them fast. And stay on them in some way that is productive.

If keeping up with schooling bass becomes a problem, or the school seems to be bobbing up and down, Grigsby suggests switching to smaller baits and slowing down, even though you may be sacrificing a great deal in casting distance. By throwing Rat-L-Traps, Tiny Traps, small finesse worms or Carolina rigged baits to the place where he saw them last, he focuses on catching fish when the school drops down.

Folkestad follows a similar procedure, utilizing a 1/8-ounce Blakemore Road Runner tied to 6-pound test on light spinning tackle or a more castable 1/2- or 3/4-ounce Hopkins spoon.

Without a certain level of confidence in nonschooling fish, the chase can become one of desperation, which Grigsby admits happens to everyone. Sometimes, concedes Grigsby, he ends up giving school bass "basically a shot with everything. But if I haven't caught them on all that, then I'm hurting."

A Clear Alternative

As in so many other bass fishing situations, schooling fish present no clear cut answer when the going gets tough. But, one "edge" to bait selection in pursuing school bass is the use of clear baits.

"If you've tried to catch them on about everything in your box, use a clear bait," offers Shaw Grigsby. "Whatever it is — topwater, jerkbait, whatever — as long as it is clear, it is extremely difficult for them to distinguish the size."

This is particularly important when the need for casting distance (i.e., larger lures like the Zara Spook) runs counter to the size of the shad. With a clear bait, especially amidst the swirling glint of a disrupted shad school, the attacking bass can only discern the vague outline of what appears to be a wounded baitfish.

Gary Klein also uses this "clear advantage" in the form of a Texas favorite, the Near Nothin'. Roughly the size of a Pop-R, this solid, clear plastic bait (equipped with a white bucktail) delivers a chugger-style action when pulled quickly across the surface. The added benefit of the Near Nothing is in its weighted midsection, which sinks the bait when the retrieve is stopped.

Using a large spinning reel, Klein casts this appropriately named lure on 10- to 12-pound test.

THERE MAY BE no better bait for schooling bass than the lipless crankbait.

TIPS FOR SHALLOW SUMMER BASS

Try these tricks for shallow water lunkers

SINCE THE PROS MADE IT POPULAR some two decades ago, deep cranking has become one of the most productive techniques for catching bass in the summertime. When the heat turns up, top pros, including David Fritts, Mark Davis and Paul Elias, hit paydirt by digging a long-billed crankbait along a deep, stumpy point or ledge — and Bassmasters seeking to emulate their heroes follow suit.

But to some fishermen, bucking trends is another route to gaining a winning edge. While their buddies are off cranking some 20-foot dropoff, these rebels revel in doing the unthinkable: fishing the shallows in the heat of summer.

On the surface, it doesn't seem like such a shocking approach. As we know, the bass is basically a shallow water critter, perfectly at home hanging around stumps and weedbeds in 2 to 3 feet of water. And haven't fishermen been catching bass shallow in summer ever since the days of the Creek Chub Wiggle-Fish and bamboo rod?

But times have changed. While it used to be no big deal to limit out on bass all summer long by merely pounding the banks, increased fishing pressure has resulted in a more savvy bass population, and a much tougher shallow bite. The result: You've got to be smarter these days if you hope to score up shallow, especially during the so-called "dog days."

Two of America's top shallow water bass experts share the following tips on finding and catching quality fish in hot, skinny water.

RIGHT AT HOME

Tennessee pro Charlie Ingram has to be adept at catching bass from all depths. But he readily admits he's most at home in the shallows, even when the water is very warm.

"I've always felt I perform best as a shallow water angler,"

**(Opposite page)
SUMMER FISH will
hold tight to cover,
making lures capable
of hitting their noses
especially important.**

Holes In Hydrilla

■ **Type of lake** — Large natural lake in Florida.
■ **Features** — Abundant emergent weeds in shallower areas and hydrilla beds in deeper water.
■ **Time of year** — Midsummer.
■ **Best pattern** — This is a time for good numbers of bass. Drift across hydrilla flats in 5 to 8 feet of water, casting to open holes with a soft plastic jerkbait or floating (weightless) worm. If these fail to produce, switch to an 8-inch plastic worm Texas rigged with a lightweight sinker, and probe the openings. Good areas to try are where the wind is rippling the surface, but where bigger waves aren't rolling.
■ **Key to success** — Home in on baitfish. If baitfish (especially shiners) are noticeable in an area, bass will be somewhere close by.

Ingram says, "and in professional bass fishing, you learn to play to your strengths. There will always be some bass in the shallows, and they'll be there regardless of how hot the water gets."

Ingram has caught big largemouth and smallmouth from shallow water topping the 100 degree mark. But he insists that not all shallow situations are conducive to holding bass during the summer season.

"If you're serious about catching quality fish up shallow in hot weather," he says, "you've got to look for the right conditions." He lists the following as paramount:

Stained water — "In summer, I have very little success finding and catching bass in clear, shallow water during the day, unless that water is chock-full of grass," he says. "Instead, I head to stained water, which might have a visibility of a couple of feet. This has sufficient clarity to allow bass to see a fairly wide array of lures and presentations, yet provides enough concealment for the fish to feel comfortable up shallow. If I can't find stained water in the right locations, I'll fish shallow, muddy water, although its decreased visibility limits the number of lures and presentations that are viable."

Forage — "Summer bass are binge feeders," Ingram notes. "They're inactive for long periods, probably to avoid being overly stressed in hot water. But they can quickly shift gears into a feeding mode, and when they do, they often stuff themselves in short order. So one of the things I look for is an abundance of baitfish close to prime, shallow holding areas. If I see a baitfish school cruising near the surface or bait flipping here and

there in the shallows, and other conditions look favorable, I'll fish that spot."

Cover — "Again, bass hold for long periods of time in hot water, and these fish like to hold close to something — a sunken tree, a weedbed, a stump. Unless they're actively feeding, I expect summer fish to be tight to cover, regardless of how deep or shallow they are. And when they do feed, they'll seldom wander far from their home base, especially if the water clarity is poor."

SHALLOW HOT SPOTS

Ingram notes some of the high percentage shallow hot spots he likes to fish in summer: "Day in and day out, big flats will be the most productive shallow areas in a slackwater reservoir during hot weather," he points out. "A flat, by definition, extends out from the bank at a very shallow slope. It might be only 2 or 3 feet deep 100 yards from the bank, and to many fishermen, it doesn't look all that fishy. But the right flat can hold large numbers of keeper bass — and some lunkers as well."

Ingram is quick to point out that not all flats are created equal. "Flats with grass cover are often the best in hot weather, since aquatic vegetation

Shallow Bass Locations

1. Dam
2. Flooded Shoreline Brush
3. Mudlike Shallow Point
4. Stumps
5. Shallow Hump
6. Big, Flat Scattered Woods, Brush, And Stumps
7. Spring-Fed Creek
8. Flat With Big Weedbed And Scattered Woods
9. Flat With Stumps And Ditches
10. Surface Pondweeds Or Scum

More Tips For Hot, Skinny Water

Charlie Ingram prefers staying shallow in summer instead of facing the frustrations of sharing water with pleasure boats on the big water. Here, he shares additional tips that can make hot, skinny water more productive.

■ **Tread lightly** — "Shallow bass are spooky, and you'll run them off if you bang your trolling motor or outboard skeg on the bottom," Ingram warns. "When fishing shallow areas, tilt your big engine up so it's not dragging through the mud, and adjust your trolling motor until it's barely in the water. Use the lowest speed you can get away with on your electric motor, or rely on the wind to drift you into position."

■ **Work outside edges** — "Summer bass are typically active only for brief periods, but they often station themselves where they can quickly spring into action should a feeding opportunity present itself," Ingram notes. "Concentrate on the outside edges of brush, stumps and shallow weedbeds, and skip the denser areas within the cover."

■ **Fish late** — Some of the best bass fishing on summer weekends takes place around 4 p.m., Ingram has found. "By this time, most of the pleasure-boaters and jet-skiers have had enough sun, so they clear out, leaving the lake calmer for fishing. This is the time to try long, shallow points with a deep water access. Fish mudlines on the point created by boat waves — sometimes bass will be in only a foot of water here."

■ **Compensate for the heat** — Take extra precautions with your bass (and yourself) in hot weather. "Don't keep any bass unless you're fishing a tournament, and then add ice to your livewell water and keep the aerators running," Ingram says. "Stick a piece of foam to the inside of the livewell lid to help insulate it. Lay a white towel over the lid when you're fishing, to reflect heat. And drink plenty of fluids."

provides ample cover, attracts a wide array of forage species and infuses plenty of oxygen into the water.

"But not all lakes have grass; in these, wood cover typically holds most of the fish. Look for laydown trees, brush and stumps." Extremely dense cover isn't necessary, Ingram adds. "Many Bassmasters have been conditioned to think that unless a flat is thick with weeds or wood, it's not worth fishing. But if it has stained water, lots of forage and at least a little cover, don't overlook it. Besides, bass are easier to target on flats that aren't overloaded with grass or wood. Bass usually gravitate to something different in their surroundings, and I've found that flats with sparse, scattered cover can often outproduce those with thick cover."

In clear lakes, Ingram looks for flats with quick access to deep water; these usually have a creek channel running along their outer edge. "In clear lakes, bass often suspend in deep water by day, then move up onto the flat under cover of darkness to feed."

Flooded shoreline bushes are another important link in Ingram's shallow summer pattern. "When a reservoir is at summer pool, thousands of bushes that were previously on dry land become inundated, and they can provide tremendous feeding opportunities for bass. Insects such as mayflies (and their larvae) are thick around these bushes,

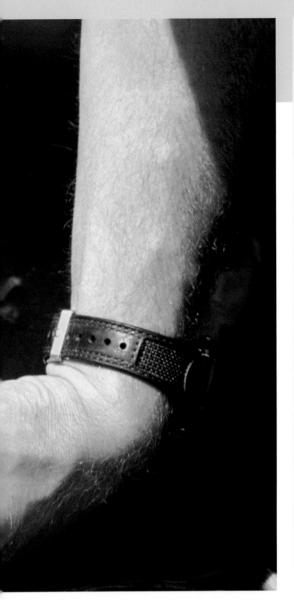

Hot Summer Lures

Choose a mix of active and less active lures for shallow summer bass. Here are the baits recommended by Charlie Ingram:

■ **Lipless crankbait** — The ultimate hot weather tournament lure for active shallow bass. Burn it whenever you see bass busting baitfish on stumpy flats.

■ **Lipped crankbait** — They work great in shallow water! Root a deep diver around stumps and logjams on flats. Finesse a shallow diver through brush and stickups. And check your line for abrasion after every cast.

■ **Buzzbait** — Arguably the best big bass lure of all in hot, skinny water . . . and not just in low light situations. Work it over shallow logjams, bump it off stumps and hang on.

■ **Spinnerbait** — The stained water marvel. Bump it against logs, flooded bushes and every stickup in sight. Light colors suggest baitfish; add a trailer to make the lure more visible in muddy conditions. Retrieve it just fast enough so you can barely see the blades flashing.

■ **Floating jerkbait** — The clearer the water, the more you need this lure. Deadly when "ripped" down a shallow weedline.

■ **Topwater popper** — The pros' choice for hydrilla and milfoil beds that top out just beneath the surface. Work it fast for active fish, then slow it way down to pull a lunker out of its weedy lair.

■ **Frog or rat** — As surface weeds and scum grow progressively denser in shallow coves, the appeal of this type of bait increases. Cut a little slit in the back and stuff the hollow lure with cut-up pieces of plastic worm to improve castability on heavy tackle. Add a couple of glass worm rattles while you're at it.

■ **Plastic worm** — Super for probing shallow brushpiles and weed edges. The key here is to use a lightweight sinker — 1/8 ounce is plenty. Try a stiff spinning outfit with 10- to 12-pound line instead of your usual hawg stick.

■ **Jig** — It's too hot to breathe. Nothing's moving. Time to flip or pitch a jig into shallow bushes, logjams and weeds. Use a pork or plastic trailer. Best colors? You can't go wrong with basic black.

drawing small predators such as bluegill, and the bass are never far behind." Ingram often catches his biggest bass from lone bushes rather than from those clumped close together.

Shallow structures swept by current can provide phenomenal bass fishing on even the hottest days.

When fishing a river-run reservoir, he'll probe deeper areas during periods of slack water, but as soon as they start generating at the upstream dam, he'll head for shallow flats, humps and points.

"Bass in river-run lakes typically time their summer feeding to the generation schedule," Ingram says. "It's not impossible to catch them when there's no current, but it's usually extremely slow fishing. The bite picks up immediately when current starts flowing. Bass 'know' that baitfish will reposition themselves in current; they take advan-

tage of a massive forage movement by gravitating to shallow places where it's easy to intercept prey."

SHALLOW SURPRISES

Shallow bass fishing can be surprisingly good in midsummer, if you follow the advice of our experts. Avoid overcrowded lakes, look for stained water, fish close to cover and follow the forage. Fish smart and you'll catch quality bass from skinny water all summer long.

WHEN BASS hide beneath impenetrable cover, frog and rat imposters should be your go-to bait.

FALL

With the dropping of leaves
and temperature comes
hot bass action …

STRATEGIES FOR COOLING WATER

Bass patterns for the transition between summer and winter

WHAT'S WRONG WITH this picture? Maybe you could forgive the slow bass bite during late summer, fishing's dreaded "dog days." But when relief comes in the form of autumn's sparkling clear days and chilly nights, most of the competition is tromping through the woods after deer or parked in easy chairs, watching football. You've got all the latest lures, fresh line on your reels and the lake to yourself, yet you still haven't tapped into that fast and furious fall bass action those fishing magazines you spent all summer reading promised you.

Two experts have stepped forth to share their secrets for finding and catching bass in cooling water: veteran Kentucky Lake guide Garry Mason and Trussville, Ala., pro Randy Howell, one of the hottest contenders on the pro circuit. Their game plans are guaranteed to make any angler's fall fishing more productive.

WHY WATER COOLS

Examining why lakes and reservoirs cool in fall is important to understanding how dropping water temperatures impact bass location and behavior, both Mason and Howell believe. They cited these reasons for the fall cool down:

Lowering air temperatures — "This is the most obvious factor impacting the temperature of the water, but not the only factor," Mason indicates. "The drop in air temperature may be gradual, or it can occur virtually overnight. A series of October cold fronts, accompanied by strong northerly winds and a sharp drop in humidity, can knock the surface temperature of the lake down 10 degrees in a week."

Shorter days, cooler nights — "These factors affect both the air and lake temperatures," Howell says. "As days grow shorter, there's less sunlight on the water, meaning a decline in plankton and weed growth. When air temperatures consistently are 15 to 20 degrees cooler at night than in the daytime, the water temp starts dropping quickly."

Fall rains — "A cold autumn rain can lower the lake's temperature in a hurry," Mason has found. "Reservoir tributaries will be the first places to cool as cold runoff enters the system. If rains persist for several days, the entire lake can undergo a rapid temperature drop, accompanied by an influx of muddy water."

SHIFTING PATTERNS, SOLID ADVICE

"Early fall can be the hardest time of the year to pattern bass," Howell admits. "Autumn is often a season of irregular weather patterns — cold one day, warm the next. You'll be wearing a down jacket and the water's still in the 70s. This can mess up your mind when it comes to locating and catching fish."

While surface temperature is always critical information, it should be taken with a grain of salt in fall, Howell cautions.

"A harsh October cold front might knock the air temp down to 42 degrees and the surface temp from 70 to 62 overnight, but if you dropped a thermometer down a few feet, you may find the

RANDY HOWELL says to look for the last available vegetation, often located near deep points, where bass will congregate in the fall.

September Spooning

■ **Type of lake** — Large, mainstream reservoir in the South.
■ **Features** — Classic structure lake with extensive flats divided by stump-lined creek and river channels.
■ **Time of year** — Early fall.
■ **Best pattern** — Bass are the deepest they'll be all year, averaging 18 feet deep on top of main lake ledges. Jig a 1/2-ounce spoon along deep dropoffs, repeatedly easing it up 6 to 8 inches off bottom, then lowering it back down. Check ledges first with a depthfinder, working ones where sonar shows fish.
■ **Key to success** — With this technique, it is imperative to fish slower and more thoroughly than when crankbaiting deep structure. When fish show on the depthfinder, be very methodical with your jigging approach.

More Tips For Fall Bass

■ Lunker bass are often most catchable during the initial stages of the fall cool-down, when they move to shallow cover adjacent to deep structural edges. Kentucky Lake guide Garry Mason catches large numbers of 6-pound-plus large-mouth when his home lake drops from around 85 to 80 degrees.

■ Average-size bass will often be most active as the lake becomes cooler. Tournament anglers frequently score limits of keepers in 75 to 68 degree water on fast moving crankbaits and spinnerbaits.

■ Bass are usually typecast as being active and aggressive in the fall, but this is often not the case. If a fast approach isn't working, slow down and saturate isolated cover with a jig or worm.

■ In many lakes, bass may undergo a forage shift as the water cools. If you aren't getting results on shad imita-tors such as silvery crankbaits and spinnerbaits, try a crawfish pattern jig or brown/orange crankbait instead.

■ Banks, coves and tributary arms facing north will usually be the first places to cool off in fall; fish are like-ly to be shallower here than else-where.

■ While small lures often produce quick limits of keepers in fall, a big bait might be your ticket to a lunker bass. Bass pro Randy Howell has taken many trophy class fish on a spinnerbait with a huge No. 7 willowleaf blade during autumn tournaments. In lakes where big bass prey on a resident trout population, try a big rain-bow-pattern crankbait or jerkbait, as cooling water sends these large forage fish shallow.

■ Lunker bass occasionally mix with packs of stripers in fall to target schooling gizzard shad. Dropping a spoon through surfacing stripers will often catch a big largemouth or small-mouth lurking beneath the school.

■ If you were catching bass in a shallow creek arm, but a fall cold front has given them lockjaw, check the creek again in late after-noon, after the sun has had time to warm the water and make fish active again.

water beneath the chilled surface band is still surprisingly warm," he notes. "Clear lakes can be slower to cool in fall than murky ones, just as they take longer to warm in spring. I often find bass well into a fall pat-tern by early October in a murky lake, but still transitioning from a summer pattern in a clear lake."

Seasonal reservoir drawdowns can further complicate fall fishing, Garry Mason says. "Most fishermen believe bass will pull out of the shal-lows as the lake level starts to drop, but shifting fall weather patterns can cause the reverse to happen. Bass may move deeper temporarily when drawdown begins, only to push back farther into the shallows as the tribu-taries cool."

"Like Garry says, bass often move shallower as the water cools in spite of lake level changes; I've found this can be the case even when the water turns muddy," Howell emphasizes. "During an October BASS tournament on Old Hickory Lake (Tenn.), the creek arms were cold and muddy after a heavy rain. I fought my instinct to fish the main lake, where the water was 10 de-grees warmer and clearer, and instead ran as far back as I could into the tributaries. Here, I found bass stacked up in incredibly shallow water — they were only 6 to 12 inches deep."

By maneuvering his boat as shallow as it would go, then making extra-long casts with small crankbaits and spinnerbaits, Howell managed to scratch out a limit every day.

A rapid influx of much-needed oxygen takes place following a fall rain, Howell adds. "At the Old Hickory tournament, as the day progressed, cold, muddy runoff poured into the creek arms and the water temperature dropped — and the bite actually got better," Howell recalls. "By noon I saw shad flipping on the surface and bass run-ning them down. I believe the runoff was high in oxygen, which activated both the baitfish and bass. A lake can become stagnant after a long, hot summer; some fresh, cool, highly oxygenated water washing into the system can rejuvenate things in a hurry."

Turnover — the phenomenon whereby water that was on the lake's bottom rises to the surface as the lake cools — can have a temporary but significant impact on fall bass patterns, Mason notes. His advice: "The water that comes to the top is low in oxygen, so until conditions stabilize, you'll find better fishing near flowing water after the lake turns over."

If a reservoir undergoes a fairly rapid drawdown while the fall season remains abnormally dry, bass tend to be on a much deeper pattern, Mason has found. "Under these conditions, they'll locate more on points and ledges at the mouths of tributaries than in the backs of the creeks. Rather than fish 1 to 3 feet deep, you may have to pull out to 8 to 12 feet and fish 'drop' lures — like a worm, a jig-and-pig or a Carolina rigged lure; you might even fish a grub or Slider worm if the water is real clear. Obviously, this requires a much slower approach than burning a crankbait, but the reward is often a big bass."

In fall, always look for isolated wood in fairly shallow water, the experts say. "Especially if it's a cast or two away from a main lake bar, creek channel dropoff or some other place where bass might congregate during the heat of summer," Mason elaborates. "The biggest fish in the pack will be the first to move up to this cover once the lake begins to cool. A stump or laydown log in 4 to 6 feet of water close to a deep structural edge can produce the trophy of a lifetime."

As fall progresses and the water temp drops

into the 50s, any seemingly insignificant stickup or piece of brush you encounter can hold a fish, Howell points out. "Most bass fishermen have been conditioned to look for cover in quantity, but in cooling water, less is more. Size doesn't matter — a bass will hunker down next to a toothpick if one is available. Bump a small crankbait into that lone branch sticking up in 2 feet of water and you'll see what I mean."

COVER PREFERENCES

Shorter days, lowering lake levels and a drop in water temperature all contribute to the die-off of

RANDY HOWELL heads for the shallows following an autumn rain shower. He believes the influx of fresh runoff gives the otherwise stagnant water an oxygen boost.

Current means cooler water and more active bass in fall, Mason indicates. "A river or river-run reservoir typically stays a lot cooler than a static body of water in the heat of summer, so naturally it's going to be cooler throughout fall as well. In some river systems, water coming from the bottom of the upstream lake might be in the 50 degree range, even in August; the temperature in the channel at the lower end of the downstream reservoir might never top 78 degrees all summer."

Anglers adept at fishing moving water often score big during the fall by targeting shallow main lake structures, such as rockpiles, humps and tapering points, rather than moving back into the creek arms.

"This is especially true for smallmouth bass, which can school up in impressive numbers on these main lake structures every autumn," adds Mason.

In late fall, when the lake is cold and fish grow lethargic, bass and their forage are attracted to the superheated water from power plant discharges.

"Bass are cold-blooded creatures and will remain in warm water whenever they can find it, regardless of the time of year," Howell says. "During a fall tournament on the Connecticut River, much of the system was only 56 degrees, but the discharge at an upstream power plant was 82 degrees. The bite was slow elsewhere, but I parked at the discharge during the entire tournament and placed seventh. All my bass were smallmouth, which aren't supposed to be all that crazy about warm water. The heated discharge was so thick with baitfish, it was like chowder."

MOST ANGLERS think bass move to deep water as a flood-control impoundment is lowered in the fall. While that is true, the fish will return to the shallows following a cold snap.

submerged and emergent vegetation in fall, our experts point out.

"Since bass derive food, shelter and oxygen from weeds, they'll stick with them to the bitter end," Howell says. "Always look for the last available vegetation, often located on deep points in the 20-foot zone in clear lakes, where light penetration is good. Root a long billed crankbait on the bottom to locate deep grass, then drop a worm or jig right into the cover — bass often bury in weedbeds during fall. When the grass is finally gone, don't panic. Bass will gravitate to wood cover next, and so should you."

PARK THE bass boat and take an autumn float down the tailwaters of a river-run reservoir. The water is cooler and the action is hotter than the lake.

EXPECT THE UNEXPECTED

As we've seen, fall is a time to expect the unexpected when it comes to bass patterns. Some fish may be in water as shallow as a tractor rut; others hanging deeper on points and ledges. Cold, muddy runoff can be as attractive to bass in one body of water as a superheated power plant discharge is in another. So keep an open mind. Fish places you may have never tried before. With patience and practice, you'll learn to crack the code on your home waters this fall.

AS WATER temperature drops, so does the activity level of largemouth. Pick your favorite worm and Texas rig it, pitching tight to cover.

Patterning Fall Bass By The Numbers

As water temperatures cool, bass patterns change. Use these guidelines from bass experts Garry Mason and Randy Howell in conjunction with a surface temperature meter to find and catch fish this autumn.

Lake Temperature	General Bass Location	Best Fishing Approach
90-80 degrees	Main lake channel structure; deep points.	Fish close to current with deep diving crankbaits and worms.
80-70 degrees	Mouth to first-third of tributary.	Target isolated wood with crankbaits, jigs and spinnerbaits. Try topwaters near creek channel edges.
70-60 degrees	Secondary points and channel bends in tributaries.	Target isolated wood with crankbaits, jigs and spinnerbaits. Don't ignore muddy runoff.
60-50 degrees	Shallow points and flats in backs of tributaries.	Try small crankbaits with tight wobble as water cools. Slow roll spinnerbaits around laydown wood. Buzzbaits can be surprisingly good now.
50-45 degrees	Stumpflats, channels and ditches in shallow tributaries.	Fish any wood cover you can find with jigs and small crankbaits. Bass are often more active late in the day, after sunlight warms the water.

DROPPING WATER
levels make bass
suspend in the fall
on Western
impoundments.

HOW TO FIND THE HOTTEST FALL ACTION

Forage is the key to fall fishing in the West

SIMILAR TO BASS FISHERIES east of the Rockies, Western lakes experience a burst of activity just before the water turns cold in late fall. This transition period often occurs later and lasts longer than it does in other regions of the country, and it provides some of the best bass action of the year on otherwise challenging Western waters.

Still, as good as fishing can be in fall, it's often tempered by the angler's own knowledge of bass' behavior on his chosen fishery.

While similar in many respects, each Western lake has unique characteristics as well. Although Shasta and Oroville are both deep and clear reservoirs dominated by spotted bass, for example, local anglers find there's a difference in how each reservoir's bass population reacts to the fall transition period. Likewise, lakes Mead and Havasu are both desert impoundments, but patterning shallow bass on each can be quite different.

Two very accomplished California pros, Gary Dobyns and Aaron Martens, possess an exceptional understanding of how unique Western bass fisheries can be. The two CITGO Bassmaster Classic participants have thoroughly dominated the Western tournament scene in their respective regions.

By considering water conditions, available cover and structure, the presence of current, forage location and movement, they are better able than most to pattern the West's various reservoirs and natural lakes in fall.

(Opposite page) AARON MARTENS probes the far reaches of tributaries for bass in the fall. He believes the bass push baitfish into these dead-end areas.

FORAGE IS THE KEY

When establishing a pattern, Dobyns first tries to determine what the bass are eating. The Yuba City angler believes it's very important to do so

Waking Up Bass

■ **Type of lake** — Deep, clear highland reservoir.
■ **Features** — Several large, winding tributary arms sport standing timber growing down sloping banks.
■ **Time of year** — Fall.
■ **Best pattern** — Lakes this time of year can be extremely clear, so the hottest fishing occurs on cloudy, windy days just prior to a frontal passage. When these conditions occur, head to the lower lake area and fish rocky banks and main lake points exposed to the wind. Cast a 1/4-ounce spinnerbait close to the bank, then retrieve it at high speed, just under the surface so it makes a wake.
■ **Key to success** — Work the windiest banks and points you can find. The wind pushes in baitfish and draws bass to the surface.

15 to 20 feet to take a jerkbait or topwater plug moving overhead. Dobyns' baits of choice are Bomber's Long A, Heddon's Zara Spook and Castaic Soft Bait's Threadfin lure. On Shasta, the spotted bass expert concentrates his search in the river arms of the popular impoundment.

Dobyns works his bait along the bank, from shallow to deep, while keeping his eye on both his electronics and the surrounding water surface as he looks for baitfish activity along the surface or suspended below. Spots and largemouth, as well as trout, will push shad to the surface. Often, when trout are feeding on the shad, large bass will be nearby feeding on the injured shad and the smaller trout.

During this period, Shasta's bass feed actively and are fairly aggressive.

"We will be fishing over some pretty deep water — 100 feet at times," adds Dobyns. "But it really doesn't matter how deep the water is, because the fish are suspended and are willing to move for a bait."

According to Dobyns, Lake Oroville anglers don't see as much topwater action in fall simply because the smelt they feed on aren't on top. "Compared to shad," he explains, "pond smelt are a deeper occurring forage fish in fall. Unlike Shasta, the key to catching quality bass on Oroville in the fall is to fish deeper."

On Lake Oroville, Dobyns spends more time jigging spoons or shaking and doodling worms for deeper bass. Typically, spots there will be found holding over structural features such as submerged points, ridges and relatively steep main lake banks in fall. "The fish can be as deep as 50 to 60 feet when they're feeding on pond smelt," explains Dobyns. "On Oroville, I am fishing deeper in fall than at any other time of year."

SHALLOW AND HUNGRY

On California's Sacramento/San Joaquin River Delta and Clear Lake, as well as Arizona's Lake Havasu, getting largemouth bass to strike a lure is not much of an issue in fall. According to Dobyns,

WHEN BASS fishing in the fall, keep a shad-type bait tied on. If you run into a feeding frenzy, cast it and hang on.

when trying to pattern the more popular spotted bass fisheries near his home. "Because Lake Shasta and Lake Oroville have differing forage bases," says Dobyns, "the predominant patterns for spotted bass often differ."

Shasta's forage is dominated by threadfin shad, while Lake Oroville's is primarily pond smelt. The spotted bass on Shasta are normally found where the schools of shad are, whether the baitfish are holding over structure or open water. Because of this, Dobyns spends most of his time looking for surface action while working reaction-type baits, such as topwaters and jerkbaits.

An accomplished tournament pro and winner of a BASS tournament on Lake Shasta, Dobyns suggests that anglers who hope to catch bass in fall must be willing to fish over suspended bass. During years of heavy precipitation, reservoir managers on many Sierra foothill reservoirs — such as Shasta, Oroville and Folsom — often drop lake levels in the fall as they prepare for runoff from winter storms.

FALL ACTION can be fast and furious if you find the baitfish. Keep a jerkbait tied on to spur the reaction bite.

The dropping water levels cause spotted bass to suspend, often over open water.

In Lake Shasta's clear water, spotted bass readily rise from depths as great as the fish in these cover-filled fisheries are aggressive and relatively shallow. Again, as similar as the three fisheries are, they differ considerably in the necessary approach.

Clear Lake has plenty of shallow cover in the form of tule-lined banks, hydrilla beds, rockpiles and man-made structures — such as boat docks and erosion abatement walls. Similar to Clear Lake, the Delta has plenty of natural cover, but feeding activity is driven by tidal influences.

On Clear Lake, Dobyns uses techniques that allow him to cover water relatively fast. "At this time of year," he explains, "you can fish pretty fast because the big fish are fairly aggressive. We do a lot of flipping and pitching, and we often fish spinnerbaits, shallow crankbaits and topwaters. The key is to cover a lot of water."

In the Sacramento/San Joaquin River Delta, largemouth bass are similarly feeding in shallow water. Of course, the biggest difference between the Delta and Clear Lake is current. "On the Delta, the fish feed along current breaks," shares Dobyns, "so I concentrate on the points in the tule berms and at the mouths of sloughs."

Although bass will feed on both incoming and outgoing tides, the falling tide tends to concentrate the fish along edges of cover, where they lie in wait for unwary prey evacuating the shallower water. Dobyns' strategy includes working topwater baits and spinnerbaits over shallow areas, and flipping and pitching worms and jigs to edges of cover. "It doesn't seem to matter whether the tide is coming in or going out," adds Dobyns, "as long as you have some tidal movement."

Aaron Martens finds shallow cover plays an important role in the fantastic bass fishing found on Arizona's Lake Havasu. While the lower portion of Havasu fishes very similar to Lake Mead, the Colorado River section is quite different. On the lower end, stripers drive shad into the grass filled coves and bays, where topwater baits and shad-imitating jigs are productive.

Upriver at the same time, bass move from the tule banks of the main channel and into the backs

Fall Bass Tactics For Highland Lakes

When conditions are right, the deep, clear lakes of the Ozarks region offer typical shallow water action for bass in the fall. However, the season's constantly changing weather can frustrate anglers at lakes like Bull Shoals and Table Rock, two clear highland reservoirs where bass quickly advance to or retreat from the shallows. While shallow water anglers must depend on this here-today-gone-tomorrow pattern, one Table Rock Lake guide probes deep water for more consistent action throughout the fall.

The depth range of fish during autumn depends on the thermocline, says guide Pete Wenners. "When the water starts to cool down, the thermocline will normally be 22 to 32 feet deep, and you usually find the fish at or just below that level," he says, noting that baitfish and spotted bass on many highland lakes remain at that depth throughout the year. In August, shad appear nearly everywhere on the main lake, but the baitfish start bunching together in the early fall before migrating into the creeks.

"Once the shad group up on the main lake, the bass also start to group, and they become a little bit easier to locate," says Wenners.

Keying on a creek or river channel also helps pinpoint bass during early autumn. Having a channel nearby makes points and flats much more productive, he adds. "If you've got a point where there's a feeder creek on one side and the main channel on the other, that's ideal. You've got good depth on both sides of the point."

Bass on these points hug the bottom near the breaklines or move out into the open water and suspend over depths of 100 to 130 feet. "Those suspending fish are some of the hardest to catch," says Wenners. "But if baitfish are suspended there as well, they become easier to catch — especially when they start feeding.

"Those bass can be kind of funny, though. If you can ever get one of them to bite, the fish will go into a feeding frenzy that might last as little as two minutes to as long as half an hour. When that happens, you can't get a bait down past them."

Wenners has developed some deep water tactics that consistently take spotted, largemouth and smallmouth bass while bank-beating anglers blank. The techniques include streaking, dragging and fluttering.

These same obscure moves can be successfully applied in the fall on other clear water impoundments throughout the country. Because they are geared toward deeper water angling, his techniques require electronic aids for tracking suspended bait and bass movements.

of the many hidden arroyos. The quiet water in the back of these vegetation-filled pockets is inhabited by baitfish, crawfish and perch. Martens recommends pitching and flipping in these backwater areas for the better fish.

Martens and Dobyns have shown that Western fisheries, although seemingly very different, are similar to Eastern bass fisheries in that fall patterns are driven by baitfish location. Because of this, anglers everywhere who are knowledgeable about bass forage have the best chance of experiencing some exceptionally hot action in fall.

SMALLMOUTH PROWLING the bank for an easy meal will annihilate a spinnerbait bumped against isolated wood in the fall.

SLING BLADES IN THE FALL
Try these autumn spinnerbait patterns

COMMON BASS FISHING PHILOSOPHY suggests that spinnerbaits are most productive in springtime. To that extent, the pages of *Bassmaster* preach the virtues of how well blade baits work in shallow water, where this weedless wonder is a dead-ringer for landing bass in both sides of the spawning cycle.

Spinnerbaits, with their blades rotating and flashing like the scales of baitfish reflected off the sunlight, imitate a small school of shad. So it only stands to reason that these shad imitators are hot baits in the fall, when bass are bulking up on forage for the winter.

BASS pro David Wharton is an advocate of using spinnerbaits in the fall, and for good reasons. Wharton's observations and experiences also tell another important story about spinnerbaits, which is: There are other fall patterns to consider in addition to simply fishing the backs of tributary creeks where baitfish are concentrated. The back-of-the-creek pattern is one of the best-known and often most reliable of all fall bass patterns. But if the creeks are crowded, muddy or simply void of fish, Wharton has plenty of other places he'll use a spinnerbait.

GRASS & BLADES

"On any lake that has vegetation, whether it's visible on the surface or not, you have potentially good spinnerbait water in the fall," he explains. "That's because vegetation provides so much of what bass of all sizes require, including food and cover.

"The key in most fall spinnerbaiting around vegetation is to stay on the edges. Sometimes this will be the deeper outside edge; other times, the inside or shallow edge. The only way you know

(Opposite page) USE A "squealing" buzzbait on quiet, calm days and a "clacker" noisemaker in choppy water.

Spinnerbaits Over The Depths

■ **Type of lake** — Deep, clear glacial lake in the North.
■ **Features** — An abundance of rocky reefs and humps.
■ **Time of year** — Fall.
■ **Best pattern** — Smallmouth bass this time of year hold on the ends of long points, rockpiles and shoals in the main body of the lake, typically at 25 to 30 feet. Work these areas with a 3/4- or 1-ounce chartreuse spinnerbait sporting a single No. 5 willowleaf blade. Cast this lure out, count it down 5 to 10 feet, then reel it back with a medium-fast retrieve. The bass will come up from deep water to take this bait.
■ **Key to success** — Work completely around a point or rockpile, trying all location/depth options to pattern the bass.

Give Fall Bass A Buzz

They may look nothing like a baitfish, but the jangling, clattering assemblage of wires and twisted pieces of metal we call buzzbaits work in the same places where baitfish swim. And they can be one of a bass fisherman's most productive lures during the fall months.

"Bass are shallow in the fall, and a lot of feeding activity takes place on or close to the surface," says veteran Florida pro Bernie Schultz. "A buzzbait streaking along the top of the water is hard for a bass to identify. It's a curiosity thing, basically. A bass may not eat a buzzbait because it's hungry, but because it has no other way to stop it except to strike it."

Buzzbaits attract bass in two ways: sound and disturbance. The swirling blades churn the surface water to a froth. They also emit two main sounds, squeaking and banging. A pass or two across the surface is enough to tell you in which category a bait belongs. And that can tell you when, where and under which conditions to work the bait.

"A blade squeaks or 'squeals' as it rubs against the rivet or a bead. With a clacker-style bait, the blade bangs against another part of the lure," Schultz, says. "The (Hildebrandt) Headbanger I use is obviously a clacker. It's made of tin, with plated blades. The difference in the sound levels between a plated blade striking tin is monumental compared to a non-plated blade striking it."

"A good rule of thumb," adds Headbanger designer Schultz "is to use a squealer on quiet, calm days, and a clacker on days when there's a little ripple on the water or in cases where you're fishing around heavy cover. The reason a clacker is better around thick cover is that it will provoke fish to give up the security of cover. It makes them chase."

which, is by fishing both edges thoroughly."

Generally, early morning and late afternoon fall fishing will be better along the inside edge, because bass have moved shallow to feed. Seeing jumping baitfish or other surface activity will help indicate whether bass are present. During the rest of the day, the outside edge often produces better. Overall, in fall, the outside edge tends to produce fewer but larger bass; the inside edge, more but smaller fish.

"On lakes where grass reaches or nearly reaches the surface, I like to fish water down to about 10 feet deep this time of year, using a 1/2-ounce tandem willowleaf, because it creates more commotion and still moves through the vegetation," he says.

"Early in the morning I start by 'bulging' or waking

the lure just under the surface, retrieving quickly and trying to cover a lot of water. The rest of the day, especially along the outside edge of a grassline, I'll slow roll the lure along the edge."

To fish the edge of a grassline this way, Wharton positions his boat on the edge itself and casts ahead, as close to the edge as he can — just as if he were fishing a shoreline. Bass will be along this edge, since it's a prime holding and ambush spot.

He especially looks for points of vegetation, channels running through the vegetation, and steeper dropoffs into deeper water. He also keeps watch for baitfish activity on the outside edge — just as he does on the inside — since it will indicate the presence of bass.

"Slow rolling is not an accurate description of how you're really fishing the lure," Wharton says, "because the lure isn't rolling over anything. Today, slow rolling has come to mean any spinnerbait retrieve that lets the lure stay deep. The only way you do that is by turning the reel handle slowly.

"When I'm slow rolling the lure over grass or along the edge, I'm simply retrieving very slowly to keep the lure at whatever depth I've chosen. Ideally, you should be able to feel when your spinnerbait begins running into grass at whatever depth. When it does, either raise your rod tip slightly or speed up your retrieve slightly so you can keep the spinnerbait just above the top of the vegetation."

SLOW ROLLING TIMBER

If a lake does not have vegetation, Wharton may consider fishing flooded timber with a standard 1/2-ounce spinnerbait fitted with No. 4 1/2 or No. 5 willowleaf blades. He'll slow roll the lure down to about 10 feet, even though the water itself may be much deeper.

"This is about as deep as you can effectively slow roll a spinnerbait and still maintain good feel and control," he explains. "Besides, when you're fishing through timber with thick branches and limbs, the less line you have out, the better.

"When fishing in big hardwoods, I want to retrieve the spinnerbait very slowly, right through the forks of the limbs. With flooded cedar trees, I'll bring the spinnerbait as close to each tree as possible, and even touch it. In either place, if a bass hits, I want to get it up and out as quickly as possible.

"There isn't much you can do to locate bass in timber except to fish a lot of it," Wharton adds. "It's always important to look for something different, like taller trees that might indicate a rise or hump, or leaning trees that show a creek channel. But most of the time you start along the outside edge and then slowly work your way in toward shallower water.

"If you start in a smaller cove, you may be able to put together the pattern more quickly. I think one of the most important things to keep in mind when you're fishing an area filled with flooded timber is that bottom configuration often becomes more important than the cover itself in actually locating bass. You need to keep an eye on your depthfinder and be alert for any depth changes."

BURNING BLUFFS

Yet another spinnerbait pattern for fall has paid off for Wharton and others when fishing deeper lakes with steep bluffs. Some call it "burning the bluffs." Wharton describes it as "rippling" the spinnerbait just under the surface and as close to the bluffs as possible. The fast moving blade bait often brings strikes from suspended bass.

"For this type of fishing, I use a 1/2-ounce spinnerbait with a single No. 6 Colorado or Indiana blade and really buzz the lure fast with my rod tip up. You make long casts and get the spinnerbait moving as soon as it touches the water — you're fishing only for reaction strikes.

"It works best in clear water, because you're targeting suspended fish that may be only a few feet below the surface. You concentrate on sheer bluffs, which frequently have a shelf extending out 10 or 20 feet down. The bass are simply holding over this shelf."

Even though grassbeds, standing timber and

WHEN AUTUMN rolls around and bass are holding on shallow cover, spinnerbaits should get the nod.

steep bluffs can provide excellent alternative fall spinnerbait patterns, the majority of today's bass fishermen will still head first to a lake's tributary creeks in hopes of catching migrating fish.

"To me, the best creeks for fishing in the fall will have some type of wood cover very near the channel itself and toward the back of the creek," says the veteran pro. "Stumps are some of the best cover, but fallen trees, brushpiles and standing timber will also attract bass. On older lakes, where the backs of the creeks may be silted in, I have found isolated cover is often better than abundant cover, and it's certainly easier to fish.

"The key to finding bass in an area like this is baitfish activity. The bait migrates into the creeks before the bass do, so there's a chance you might actually be there ahead of the bass. I like water 2 to 3 feet deep, and I use a 1/4-ounce spinnerbait with a willowleaf blade behind a smaller Colorado. All I do is keep my boat in the deeper channel and cast to either side, slowly rolling the spinnerbait around the cover and over the drop."

In the South, fall spinnerbait patterns like these begin to develop in September after the first two or three fronts drop water temperatures into the 70s. Farther north, the patterns may begin developing slightly earlier. The best fishing takes place in October and continues as late as December in some areas.

SPINNERBAITS come in a multitude of sizes and colors. And all of them work, if you customize your selection to the conditions.

WINTER

Make bass fishing
a year-round pastime
by understanding winter habitat …

TRICKS FOR DEEP FREEZE BASS

Jig one of these lures for deep holding bass in winter

IT WAS BEGINNING to look a lot like Christmas the December morning Bob Tyndall went bass fishing on Table Rock Lake. But more than the holiday spirit filled the air as he ventured out on the southwest Missouri reservoir.

Tyndall had his doubts about catching any fish that day, as a cold front had swept through the area the previous night, dropping the air temperature to 27 degrees and leaving behind a stiff breeze and an overcast, snow laden sky. Despite these conditions, he remained confident the bass would be biting.

His intuition was right — the only problem he had in catching fish was keeping the ice out of his rod tips. During the eight hour trip, Tyndall caught nearly 80 black bass, including 30 keepers (15 inches or longer). Most of the fish were spotted bass, but he also landed a 4-pound largemouth and a couple of keeper smallmouth.

(Opposite page) USE A vertical presentation in the same areas you fish during the summer for hot wintertime action.

While wintertime cold fronts can shut down fishing for some anglers, Tyndall overcomes this problem by concentrating on bass in deep water.

"Fronts don't affect those fish nearly as much as shallow fish," says the guide who formerly held the record for the largest bass caught in a BASS tournament (a 12-13 largemouth he caught in the St. Johns River during the 1973 Florida Invitational).

Even if he has to break through ice at the ramp, he can consistently catch deep water bass throughout the winter.

"It seems that when the water temperature drops to around 55 degrees, bass will school up," says Tyndall, who notices this occurring on Table Rock in early November. By December, the water temperature drops into the low 50s or mid-40s and bass bunch up near the bottom at

Schools Of Scattered Shad

■ **Type of lake** — Deep, clear highland reservoir.
■ **Features** — Several large, winding tributary arms sport standing timber growing down sloping banks.
■ **Time of year** — Midwinter.
■ **Best pattern** — Head upstream on the main tributary and look for long channel swing points that run far out into the lake. Bottom depths should be 45 to 55 feet. Cruise and watch the depthfinder for small, scattered schools of shad. Work these areas by vertically fishing a 3- to 5-inch skirted grub rigged on a 5/16-ounce jighead. Lower the bait to the bottom, then raise it 3 to 6 inches and shake it gently.
■ **Key to success** — If you see big schools of shad on the depthfinder, go somewhere else. If bass are present and feeding, these shad will be scattered.

flats. Another area where he finds schooling bass is a dropoff next to a long gravel point.

"If they aren't on the gravel close to the bottom, they'll be fairly close to it but suspended right over the channel, feeding on shad," says Tyndall. "If they are not there, just move farther out. A lot of times you'll find them over a spot where it drops off deeper (60 to 80 feet). The fish will still be out there suspending, with the shad around 50 feet deep."

In addition to the structure, Tyndall also searches for baitfish activity on his Lowrance X-16 paper graph. The guide generally avoids areas loaded with big schools of shad, though. "I normally look for little bunches of shad that are suspended off the bottom a little," he says. "You don't have to have any shad showing up, though, to get the fish to bite."

Unlike most deep water experts, Tyndall forgoes the traditional marker buoy to pinpoint schools. Buoys draw attention from other anglers, he believes, and besides, the fish tend to move around on the structure.

Instead, when he finds a school of bass and baitfish activity, he constantly monitors his paper graph, doing his best to stay on top of the school. "As long as I am seeing fish and getting bites, I know I'm still over them," he says.

Even if bass fail to appear on sonar, Tyndall won't leave certain spots without dropping a lure to the bottom. On numerous occasions, he has moved across a flat without seeing any fish on the graph, yet when he dropped his lure over the side, the device showed bass moving up to intercept the falling bait.

"They'll come up and hit the lure before it ever reaches the bottom," says Tyndall, who notices that other anglers run over an area and leave if they don't see any fish on their electronics. "The bass are there, and they're there big time."

Tyndall also camps on a spot he thinks has potential. "You have to stay with it for a little while to give the fish a good chance to bite," he adds. "If

AVOIDING HUGE schools of shad in favor of smaller concentrations will pay big dividends during winter.

depths of 50 to 55 feet. They remain there until mid-January, when they start suspending at 20 to 25 feet.

When searching for schooling bass in deep water, Tyndall recommends moving a long distance from the bank. "People will think you're crazy because you're so far away from the bank," he says. "On any deep highland lakes, where you have lots of fields running out to the channels and little gullies, just look for flats that have 50 to 55 feet of water over them."

He finds bass quickly along these vast stretches of water by targeting the ditches and gullies in the

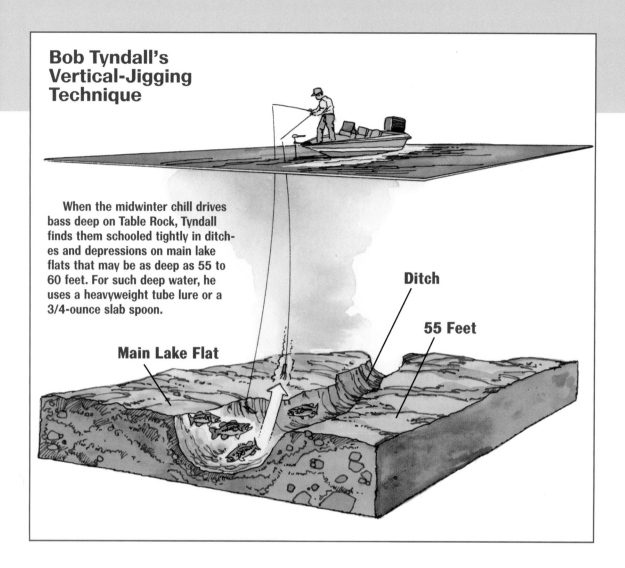

Bob Tyndall's Vertical-Jigging Technique

When the midwinter chill drives bass deep on Table Rock, Tyndall finds them schooled tightly in ditches and depressions on main lake flats that may be as deep as 55 to 60 feet. For such deep water, he uses a heavyweight tube lure or a 3/4-ounce slab spoon.

Ditch

55 Feet

Main Lake Flat

they turn on, you can really put a lot of fish in the boat. It may be a matter of an hour or two through the day when you can catch fish that quickly; the rest of the time, you're just fishing."

Whether he's concentrating on bass suspended or clinging to the bottom, Tyndall positions his boat over the top of the fish and presents his lures vertically. The most productive lures for his wintertime techniques include a Fat Gitzit, a plastic grub, 4-inch finesse worm, Rapala Balanced Jigging Lure and a slab spoon.

For aggressive bass, Tyndall relies on a 1/2- to 3/4-ounce Hopkins Shorty spoon or a Hawgjaw slab spoon in chrome, white, brass or coffee hues. He typically jerks the lure a couple of feet off the bottom and lets it fall to trigger a strike. He favors working the spoon with 17- to 20-pound-test line and a 6- to 6 1/2-foot, medium heavy to heavy action rod with a limber tip.

When bass become finicky, Tyndall resorts to the finesse plastic baits, such as the 4-inch worm, grub or tube jig. On certain days, bass seem to prefer the extra tail action provided by a plastic grub, so Tyndall sticks a 3- or 5-inch Yamamoto or Kalin's grub on a darter-style jighead. He also rigs the finesse worm on a darter jighead, which Tyndall prefers over a round jighead because it gives both the finesse worm and the plastic grub a more realistic look.

The lure Tyndall relies on the most throughout winter is the Fat Gitzit. Anytime he's working the tube jig deeper than 40 feet, Tyndall sticks the plastic tube body on a 5/16-ounce round jighead. His tackle includes a 6- to 6 1/2-foot, medium action spinning rod and a spinning reel with a large line capacity, which helps alleviate line memory.

In most situations, Tyndall uses either 8-pound Maxima or Berkley XT green line, but when the

LOOK FOR **flats surrounded by deep water where wintertime bass will school along the ledges.**

try to make it undulate just a little," Tyndall explains. He continues to shake the rod tip so the lure undulates in front of a bass — eventually teasing it into striking.

If the shaking technique fails to produce, Tyndall lets the lure drop to the bottom and then slowly reels it up while watching his sonar graph. "I'll see the fish coming up underneath it, so I just keep the lure coming. They just eat it."

On other occasions, Tyndall raises his rod to shoulder level, causing the tube jig to slowly climb 5 to 6 feet off the bottom. Again, he expects bass to follow the tube. If they don't take it, he shakes the bait gently in its raised position. If nothing strikes at that point, he lets the bait fall back to the bottom, and that usually does the trick.

fishing gets tough, he scales down to low visibility Maxima 6-pound-test monofilament. His primary tube bait colors for the clear waters of Table Rock include any hues resembling a shad, such as salt-and-pepper, gray-and-black flake or clear with blue, silver and red flakes.

The slower fall and subtle action of the Fat Gitzit make it an irresistible lure even for sluggish bass. "When those bass aren't feeding very well, if you take a spoon or something else moving up and down fast, they are just not aggressive enough to hit it," says Tyndall. "With this bait, you can keep it right on their nose and it's easy for them to get."

A simple retrieve works best for the tube jig. After letting the lure drop to the bottom, Tyndall cranks the reel handle one turn and then starts shaking his rod tip.

"You should jerk the lure;

When he feels a tap, Tyndall waits for the bass to "load up" on the lure before setting the hook. "If you set the hook too quickly, you'll often miss the fish," says Tyndall, who likes to let the fish hold the lure for a couple of seconds before he sets the hook. If he feels a strike when he has his rod at shoulder level, he drops the rod down and quickly reels up slack before trying to drive the hook into the fish's mouth.

If the bite slows down in an area, Tyndall changes colors of his tube bait to get bass active again.

Fat Gitzits and plastic grubs produce more bites, but when Tyndall wants to catch a quality bass, he switches to the Rapala Balanced Jigging Lure, a bait originally designed for ice fishing. The lure falls in the same fashion as a Gitzit and can be presented with the same shaking or lifting/lowering sequence as the tube bait.

Since bass tend to slam this lure, Tyndall resorts to heavier tackle: a medium action baitcast rod

DOWNSIZING IS always smart when the temperature dips. Try a straight-tail worm on a jighead for cold weather bass.

and a reel filled with 10- or 12-pound-test line. The guide also sets his drag loosely to absorb the hard hit a bass inflicts on the ice bait. Tyndall notices that a lot of bass are poorly hooked when they attack the lure, and the hooks might pull out if the drag is set too tight.

The lure has produced several quality bass, including an 8-pound largemouth, for Tyndall during the winter. "You'll catch a lot of largemouth in the 5- to 6-pound range on this lure," the guide says.

Big bass like that are ample reasons to take a break from the holiday rush and brave the cold on your favorite highland reservoir. But be warned, steady action on schooled bass can be addictive. Before you know it, you'll be behind on your Christmas shopping chores.

Superhot Fishing In Power Plant Lakes

When most bass fishermen are parked beside the fireplace dreaming of springtime, some anglers are literally electrified by the idea of bass fishing when the water temperature plummets into the 40s.

Power plant lakes — those that operate with hot water discharge systems — could banish those fishing blues permanently, if only you knew what these anglers have learned through the years. Their secrets of success on power plant lakes and rivers can recharge your own fishing strategies, not only during late fall and winter, but all year long.

North Carolina's David Fritts, the legendary BASS points–race holder and world champion angler, has fished virtually all types of lakes that use water for cooling.

"The main thing I've discovered everywhere I've fished is that each of these systems creates current," he says. "If the intake is located in one creek while the plant discharges into another, you'll sometimes have several miles of shoreline affected by current. And current always creates better fishing. This is true even in lakes where power plants simply generate power and create current without discharging hot water.

"When fishing power plant lakes, I look for eddies near the intake or the discharge. When current is swift, eddies are key. Farther from the intake or discharge — where current diminishes somewhat — home in on underwater points, sandbars or bridge pilings, anything that catches current and where bass can hide.

"Fifty or 60 degree water is just about perfect," Fritts adds, "but you can find willing fish even when water is cooler. Of course, cooler water means slower fish. Try slow rolling a 1/2-ounce spinnerbait to produce strikes in cooler water."

Fritts' strategy is dependent on water color, too. "If water's clear or clearing — especially in spring — I'll start out with a No. 7 shad-colored Shad Rap. Sometimes the bass will want a larger or smaller size, but if I had to choose just one, it would be a No. 7. In off-colored water, try a jig-and-pig in black-and-brown, black-and-blue or black-and-chartreuse. Bite a Zoom Trick Worm in half and use the tail as your trailer, or use a chartreuse salt chunk for that extra flash bass love."

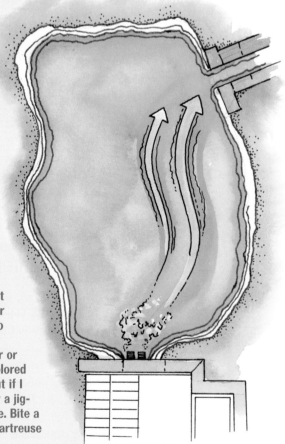

KEEP AN eye on the electronic graph for baitfish activity where largemouth hold on main lake points and humps.

DEEP WATER TACTICS FOR WINTER LARGEMOUTH

With the right lures, you can catch huge bass in the dead of winter

WITH PERHAPS THE BIGGEST largemouth bass in Oklahoma on the line, Chuck Justice was hogtied.

The only man ever to have three bass on Oklahoma's top 20 lunker list, Justice was fishing a deep point at McGee Creek Reservoir on a brutally cold Saturday in February. He and his client were on big fish — 5 pounds and up — but a local tournament in progress had them playing close to the vest. If anyone saw either of them so much as snap a wrist, boats would flock to this place like gulls to a chum line.

And so it happened that a boat approached as Justice helplessly watched his line slice across the water. Instead of setting the hook, he lowered his rod and tried to appear bored.

When Justice finally raised his rod tip, he felt tension, and yanked. A substantial force on the other end surged deep, and Justice thought he had hooked a big catfish. Then, as often happens, the line went slack as the fish raced toward him. Seconds later, the biggest bass Justice had ever seen launched skyward, tail walked and then threw the lure like a slingshot.

The man who has caught or led clients to more than 100 largemouth heavier than 10 pounds on Lake Fork, McGee Creek Reservoir and neighboring Sardis Lake, suddenly felt ill, for the grandest Sooner bass of all had just done a Houdini.

On the other hand, it was the perfect example of how exciting icebox bass fishing can be — if Justice were to break the state record, there couldn't have been a better day to do it.

In the dead of winter, in the wake of a cold front?

Absolutely. On days when anemic half-limits of tail-touchers win local tournaments, Justice, a guide specializing in giant largemouth, consistently leads his clients to some of the biggest bass of their lives. All it takes are a few specific lures, an acute understanding of winter bass behavior and a tremendous amount of discipline.

The first and most important step, Justice says, is picking the right spots.

"Basically, in the wintertime I key on two types of areas," he explains. "I like to stay in the main lake and key on humps and points. At McGee Creek, for example, there is a lot of 80- to 100-foot-deep water. I'll stop in about 60 feet and get the trolling motor on the lowest speed I can use."

LOCATING WINTER BASS

Using his Lowrance electronic graph, Justice follows the point in a straight line, from deep to shallow, marking fish. He says he usually marks one group of fish between 8 and 12 feet deep and another close to the bottom. The first group is shad, and the deeper group is bass. Bass in that situation don't rise to the shad, he notes. Instead, they hover below and eat the dead and dying baitfish that flutter down from the school.

This is where it gets dicey, for a careless mistake will spook the bass and ruin the fishing before you can make a cast. A quiet, cautious approach virtually guarantees nonstop action for as long as it lasts.

"As I go over fish, I wait until I get past them and no longer see them on the depthfinder," Justice says. "I'll drop a marker buoy, and then I'll go half a cast past the marker buoy and drop anchor. If the boat is in 12 to 18 feet, I'll cast out to about 40 feet."

Keeping an eye on the buoy is extremely important, Justice emphasizes, because bass in cold water usually concentrate around very small, subtle pieces

Structure Fishing For Giants

■ **Type of lake** — Western water storage reservoir.
■ **Features** — Small canyon impoundment known for huge bass.
■ **Time of year** — Winter.
■ **Best pattern** — This is the prime season for catching big bass on Western lakes. To try for them, fish main lake points, humps and ledges down to 40 feet. Locate bass electronically by scanning likely structure with a fish locater. When fish are found, cast a 3/8-ounce jig-and-pig. For greater numbers of smaller fish, jig a 1/2- or 3/4-ounce Hopkins spoon vertically over the school, or "doodle" with an 8-inch worm.
■ **Key to success** — Don't stop to fish a spot unless large returns are showing up on the depthfinder. Also, be diligent to set the pattern in terms of the fish's depth, which can change daily.

A GRUB rigged to a jighead is one of the baits used by winter trophy hunter Chuck Justice.

A TAILSPINNER and elongated grub are two of Justice's secret winter weapons.

of structure. Missing the target zone by a few feet can mean the difference between spectacular success and futility.

"There's always going to be something on that point the fish gather around," Justice says. "It may only be 20 feet in diameter — a pile of boulders or something — but once you get a hit in that area, you'll catch a fish on every cast. If you get outside that area, you won't get a single bite."

Finding the fish is only the beginning. Getting them to bite is another matter altogether. However, you can simplify the process by using a few basic lures perfectly suited to largemouth anchored over deep structure.

"I've got four baits for this situation," Justice says, "and on any given day, one of those baits will catch fish."

STANDUP GRUBS

The first is a Gene Larew grub on a Gene Larew standup jighead. Justice prefers watermelon, pumpkin/green and smoke/silver. This is the simplest and easiest option to use. Bass will either hit it on the drop, or they'll hit it as you drag it slowly across the bottom.

The second option Justice recommends is the

Gene Larew Long John. It resembles a Sassy Shad, except without the protruding belly, and it has more of a side-to-side motion than does the Sassy Shad. The key to catching fish is to work it very slowly, which requires rigging it with a light jighead. Justice prefers to use 1/4 ounce, and he never goes heavier than 3/8 ounce.

"One of the keys to catching fish in the winter is that you have to fish real slow," Justice says. "To fish the Long John, you make a real long cast and let it fall on free spool to the bottom. Once you begin catching fish, you have to start watching your line. If it normally takes a count of 25 for it to get to the bottom, but stops after a 10-count, that's because a fish has come up and taken it."

Once the lure hits bottom, Justice drags it in short bursts no longer than the width of his shoulders. The same tactic applies when using the skirted grub. The reason, he explains, is because strikes usually occur while the bait is moving. If you sweep your shoulders too far, you'll be out of position for a good, strong hook set, and that will prevent you from catching big bass.

"The instant you feel the tap, set the hook. If you do miss the fish, don't pull the bait up. Many times, another fish will take the bait before it hits the bottom, or just as it hits. I think the bass get excited when another fish misses a lure. Sometimes I'll get three or four strikes before I actually get the hook into one."

The Lure Of Ice Fishing

As winter settles in, bass anglers in places like the Northeast and upper Midwest keep a close eye on the lakes and waterways for signs of ice. They know that bass lurk beneath the ice, and that the eating then is just as good as it is in the summertime. When ponds and streams are frozen, some of the best fishing holes are accessible by snowmobile and snowshoe.

You don't need a bass boat because you can walk on — even drive on — ice to your favorite fishing spot. It's not unusual to see more cars on a lake in winter clustered around a "hot" fishing hole than you'd see boats there in summer.

Ice augers, tents, warming huts and clothes have reached sophisticated proportions in dealing with the only enemies of the winter angler: ice and cold. It all adds up to an extended fishing season for dedicated bass anglers.

To catch bass under ice, you should know the location of a half-dozen holes that typically hold bass when a body of water isn't frozen. This may take some preliminary scouting during summer and fall months. To find such holes, cruise along in a boat very slowly where the water is calm and clear. Look for a hole more than 20 feet deep

FOR ICE fishing action, fish over the same areas that produce in summer.

adjacent to a sharp dropoff, not far from a submerged weedbed.

Rods and reels specially designed for icy weather conditions are available, as is ultralight fishing line (ice angling experts suggest using very light monofilament line, no more than 4-pound test), and lures made specifically for ice fishing. A useful item is a tip-up, which is a device made out of wood or plastic that has a spool of line which tips up a flag when a fish is on it, hence the name tip-up. This enables an angler to fish with more lines than he or she can actually hold.

Whether you use natural bait or artificial lures, jigging through the ice is quite different from jigging in open water. Of course, no cast is made. Instead, the lure is simply lowered through a fishing hole and allowed to sink to the bottom. Then it's raised and lowered constantly, the aim being to keep the lure moving.

To get the attention of cold weather largemouth, you need to put your offering right in front of their noses. You have some leeway using this method, since wintertime bass tend to gather in large schools and suspend vertically rather than horizontally.

THE SECRET WEAPON

The secret weapon in Justice's tacklebox is an obscure lure called the Spinner Bug. Made by Weedless Lures, the Spinner Bug is an adaptation of the legendary Little George tailspinner. The main difference is that the line runs through the lead body and attaches to the treble hook independently, making it perfect for areas with thick cover, such as Lake Fork. In fact, Justice says it's the one lure he'd feel comfortable using on any lake.

"It's really a neat little bait," Justice says. "The body is independent of the hook, kind of like a slip sinker, so if a bass comes out of the water and jumps, it won't throw the hook — the weight goes up the line and doesn't eliminate any leverage. When you look at it, you think you'd get hung up every cast, and sometimes you do. But all you have to do is get over it and pop your line. That sliding weight is just like having a plug knocker on your line."

PATIENCE IS THE KEY

Finally, the most important key to successful winter bass fishing is to be patient. If you can find fish, Justice insists, you can catch them. It just takes the right lure and the right presentation.

"The more casts you have to make to catch a fish, the bigger that fish will be. If I have to make 10 casts to catch a fish, that's when I catch one of those 9- or 10-pounders. I may stay on a spot for an hour or more, but on the positive side, I don't have to do a lot of running around."

And, as Justice will readily tell you, it's not easy holding your bluff when a record-book largemouth is on the line.

DEEP BASS aren't difficult to catch — if you can find them. Once located, however, they are easily fooled by a jigging spoon or lead-head soft plastic bait.

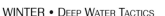

HOW TO STAGE A FRONTAL ASSAULT

Don't despair when a brutal front throws cold water on your fishing plans. Take these experts' advice for finding cold front bass

FRIDAY, 7 P.M. You're busy getting your boat and tackle ready for tomorrow's bass club tournament. The weather has been mild and muggy all week. You're confident tomorrow's bass bite will be strong.

Saturday, 1:15 a.m. You're awakened by thunderclaps. You look out your window to see rain blowing sideways as a violent storm moves through. Will this mess up your fish catching pattern?

Saturday, 4:00 a.m. Your alarm goes off and you hurriedly get dressed. Upon stepping outside, frigid air slaps you in the face — the wind has shifted out of the north and the air temperature has plummeted to 37 degrees. Stars light up the night as you drive to the lake. By the time you get to the truck stop to meet your partner for breakfast, the temperature on the gauge outside reads 32 degrees, and your confidence level has dropped accordingly.

Another tournament . . . another cold front! At times it seems as though the weatherman has it in for us poor bass anglers. Why is it that a frontal passage always seems to blow our way just before a bass tournament or a much anticipated fishing trip?

Few events can shatter a Bassmaster's confidence like a cold front. When one blows through, many anglers simply throw in the towel. Others may tough out the chilly winds and frigid temperatures for a spell, but their hearts aren't in it. After all, what's the use? Everybody knows a cold front gives bass a major league case of lockjaw, right?

There are steps you can take to find and catch bass in spite of seemingly adverse conditions. If you've ever felt your confidence level drop during a frontal passage, read and heed the information that follows. It'll give you the ammunition you need to stage a "frontal assault" of your own.

MYTHS & MISCONCEPTIONS

"Fishermen have created many myths and misconceptions about what happens to bass during a cold front," believes Doug Hannon, who has spent almost as much time under the water as he has on it, and knows firsthand that bass aren't victimized by cold fronts nearly to the extent anglers commonly believe. "Once you understand what really happens to bass during a frontal passage,

your ability to catch them, and your confidence level, will improve dramatically," he declares.

What weather changes are typically manifested by a cold front? Hannon lists the following:

Clearing skies and increased light levels — "A frontal passage is often marked by clouds and rain giving way to bluebird skies."

Lowered humidity and increased ultraviolet light levels — "The high humidity typical of prefrontal conditions acts as an effective filter of ultraviolet light. As the front passes and humidity drops, this filter is dissipated and more UV light reaches the earth."

Barometric pressure changes — "The pressure shifts downward as the front approaches, then rises once it passes."

Postfront Finesse

■ **Type of lake** — Large natural lake in Florida.

■ **Features** — Abundant emergent weeds in shallower areas and hydrilla beds in deeper water.

■ **Time of year** — Winter.

■ **Best pattern** — Winter in Florida can be very good for bass fishing, but only if northern cold fronts aren't blowing through. If weather is favorable and the water temperature is 64 degrees or higher, bass may start spawning as early as December in central Florida. A strong front will move fish off the beds. In that case, fish finesse baits (worms, tubes and crawfish) in the nearest thick cover to the spawning flats.

■ **Key to success** — Stay on the move when searching for active beds. When you find one, chances are others will be nearby.

A shift in wind direction — "Often the wind shifts 180 degrees from south to north."

Dropping air temperatures — "The temperature drop can be extreme. One December during a fishing trip in Tennessee, a cold front blew through. The high was 59 degrees one day, only 28 the next."

Dropping water temperatures — "Frigid winds can quickly chill the surface layer and shallows of the lake."

How do bass react to these changes? "They aren't knocked out of commission by them as most fishermen assume," Hannon insists.

"Bass are tough and resilient predators, not victims of changing weather. But in a sense, they're realists, too — they can tell when feeding opportunities will be good, and when they're likely to be poor." One way cold-blooded creatures like bass live a long life is by conserving their energy during cold front conditions, Hannon explains. "Rather than expend a lot of energy prowling in vain for forage, they 'chill out' and sit tight until feeding conditions improve."

Bass "read" the weather changes accompanying a frontal passage in much the same way a motorist reads traffic signs, Hannon says. "Most fishermen believe that many of the changes accompanying a cold front, especially increased sunlight and UV light levels, somehow irritate the bass and make it physically uncomfortable. I can assure you the bass is a lot tougher than that! Rather, bass read these weather changes as a sign that feeding probably won't be very good for a while. They respond by either moving tighter to cover, or deeper."

Why isn't feeding likely to be very successful in cold front conditions? "Some of the weather changes typical of a passing front have a definite effect on the bottom of the food chain," Hannon notes. "Small, fragile creatures, including terrestrial insects inhabiting the perimeter of the lake, aquatic insect larvae, fish fry and tiny crustaceans, can indeed be adversely affected by a frontal passage. They're impacted by plunging air and water temperatures, increased solar and UV penetration, etc. When these creatures stop moving around actively, small fish which feed upon them go into a holding pattern, and this in turn puts a damper on the larger predators in the food chain, including bass. When weather conditions stabilize in a few days and conditions improve, the food chain kicks into high gear again."

LOCATING BASS IN COLD FRONTS

Hannon, an accomplished diver and underwater photographer, has documented bass on film and videotape during cold fronts, and offers these tips on locating fish: "The most critical question to answer is, 'How deep?' Bass want a safe place where they can lie low for a period of time during frontal conditions. As a rule of thumb, if the shallow margin of your home lake has plenty of submerged vegetation and/or dense wood cover, bass are likely to remain shallow. But if the shallows lack thick cover, bass typically move deeper, where it's easier for them to keep a low profile — 10 to 12 feet is adequate in most lakes."

Hannon knows shallow, cover-oriented bass are the easiest to catch during a cold front. "But these fish can be easily overlooked by anglers. They often bury in the thickest cover and won't bite unless you drop a lure right in front of their noses." This is where flipping and pitching pay off big, he adds. "Dense cover evidently gives bass a tremendous sense of security, for you can usually move your boat right on top of the fish and use a short-line presentation to get them to bite. A jig and a plastic worm are my two top lure choices when bass are on a shallow cold front pattern."

Deeper fish require a bottom bumping approach.

WHEN THE COLD front hits, pitch a weighted tube tight to cover. An ultra-slow retrieve may be the only way to generate bites.

Dam

Hollow Where Bass Suspend

Bank With Deep Access (Summer)

Isolated Stump

Standing Timber

Tree

Stumps

Hump

Matted Vegetation (Summer/Fall)

Green Weeds

"If a bass moves around 8 feet deeper in response to cold front cues, its swim bladder compresses, causing it to temporarily lose its flotation ability. I've photographed bass on deep ledges with their bellies to the bottom — when alarmed, they swim right along the bottom. They'll still eat, but they aren't going to chase down a fast moving target, especially one swimming through open water. Crawl a jig slowly along the bottom if you want to get bit."

NEW ATTITUDE

Like most blowhards, a cold front's bark is often worse than its bite. Next time a front blows through and those cold winds howl, don't back down — hit the water with confidence. Be patient. Maintain a positive outlook. Do the right things, and you'll connect with bass.

Where Ron Shuffield Catches Cold Front Bass

Bismarck, Ark., pro Ron Shuffield maintains a positive attitude when faced with a frontal situation. "I assume the bite will be slower, and adjust my presentation accordingly," he advises. Here's where Shuffield looks for bass:

■ **Standing timber** — "In deep lakes, bass often suspend in 'pole timber' standing on the edge of creek or river channels. A spoon is an obvious lure choice, but also try a big jig with a fat pork chunk free-lined into the trees — this will sink slower and can draw strikes from sluggish fish."

■ **Stained water** — "I have better luck catching bass in cold fronts from moderately stained water than from either clear or muddy water. In a very clear lake, look for stained water running into the lake from tributary arms, or fish deeper, where visibility is diminished. Avoid muddy lakes during cold fronts."

■ **Submerged grass** — "Not always available, but when it is, I fish it hard. Look for isolated clumps of grass, and for the last remaining green grass in late fall."

■ **Stumps, logs, trees** — "Fish very tight to these objects. Bass will hunker down right next to them during a frontal passage."

■ **Breaklines** — "Critical places to fish, especially in a shallow lake. Bass will often move to the first breakline adjacent to shallow bays and flats, and hold there until weather conditions stabilize. A drop of 1 or 2 feet is sufficient to attract them."

■ **Overhead cover** — "Bass love to get under lily pads, matted hydrilla, water hyacinths and other surface cover during a frontal passage."

■ **Subtle structures** — "During a cold front, the Bassmaster who really knows the lake can score big. During low water periods, note the location of little ditches, depressions, high spots and other seemingly insignificant places that most anglers overlook. Bass often bunch up on them during cold fronts."

■ **Banks close to deep water** — "I especially like these during a summer cold front. Bass sulking in deep water will be energized by the drop in temperature and move to the closest bank to feed."

SMALLMOUTH PATTERNS

Master the quirks of the gamest
bass that swims …

EARLY SEASON SMALLIES

Water can't be too cold for big bronzebacks

THERE ARE TWO WIDELY accepted notions for dealing with premature spring bassin' fever: Go fishing to work out winter's kinks and perhaps stumble onto a largemouth, or sit tight until warm sunshine simmers water temperatures into the high 50s. However, there is a third and better option for anglers who are privileged to fish lakes that contain both smallmouth and largemouth.

Most fishermen know that mid- to upper-50 degree water triggers bass activity, but few acknowledge the fact that smallmouth thrive in cold water and will spawn long before the largemouth. Anglers who make smallies a priority increase their productivity during the winter-to-spring transition.

For some reason, most don't. Perhaps they're preoccupied with notions of lunker largemouth, or maybe they assume the smallmouth is too difficult to catch and requires more patience than they care to give. That may be true at certain times of the year, but not early spring, reason savvy smallmouth anglers like Jerry Gras, president of Hogan Pro Baits in Holland, Mich.

Most of Gras' early season smallmouth locations are shallow ledges adjacent to dropoffs with scattered rocks, brush and a few weeds that survived the winter. Throughout the Great Lakes watershed, and especially river-fed fisheries, there is an abundance of smallmouth and largemouth.

Some of Gras' hot spots are adjacent to deep water, but that isn't a prerequisite for early smallies. Some of his biggest smallmouth come off rocky banks a couple hundred yards or more from deep water.

"I think they spawn near there and use that rocky bank for feeding," he says. "The rocky shore

SMALLMOUTH experts agree that two key factors influence early season smallmouth success: spawning areas and the inside turns of steep dropoffs.

adds warmth to the water and attracts food. It's a spot I check several times a day."

If the area can be fished with exposed-hook jigs, such as Gitzits or Twister-Tail grubs, Gras doesn't hesitate. Otherwise, he'll try Rapalas twitched or cranked slightly beneath the surface, or a spinnerbait that throbs along the bottom.

Gras isn't alone in his early smallmouth quest. Northern Indiana's Greg Mangus fishes smallmouth any time open water is available.

"I've had big smallmouth dancing on their tails in 3 feet of 34 degree water, when ice still covered part of the lake," said Mangus.

He admits that fishing is far better when water temperatures reach the 40s, with the best action beginning at 45 degrees. Although fishing can be

sporadic, it's very predictable once water temperatures touch 48 degrees, he adds.

"You'll find them bunched up in areas — places that hold them year after year — and can catch them all day long," he says. "My biggest smallmouth of the year are caught during early prespawn periods."

An experience that illustrates his point occurred one February at Pickwick and Wilson lakes in Alabama. One day, while fishing Pickwick, he and a friend caught and released 11 smallmouth that weighed 55 pounds. On Wilson the next day, their first four bass weighed 26 pounds!

"The locals said it was too early for the smallmouth, but the water temperature seemed right based on what happens in the North later," he recalls.

Blades For Reef Bass

■ **Type of lake** — One of the five Great Lakes.

■ **Features** — Huge natural lake lined with bays and dotted with rock reefs.

■ **Time of year** — Midspring.

■ **Best pattern** — With the water temperature in the low to mid-40s and rising, smallmouth feed actively in preparation for spawning. Use charts and a depthfinder to find reefs, rockpiles and shipwrecks in 20 to 40 feet of water. Fish the upwind side with 1/4- to 1/2-ounce metal-blade baits. Cast ahead of the boat and let the bait settle to the bottom, then pull the bait 4 to 6 inches off bottom before lowering it again.

■ **Key to success** — It may be necessary to anchor or use a drift sock to hold position in high waves.

BURN spinnerbaits across shallow spawning flats adjacent to deep water.

"All I did was apply the seasonal pattern I learned in the North to what I saw there, and it worked. There's no such thing as a Yankee smallmouth and a Rebel smallmouth. They're the same, and they do what they gotta do based on the season."

Mangus says there are two key factors to early spring smallmouth locations: Nearby spawning areas and inside turns of steep dropoffs. Put the two together and you've got an early spring hot spot.

On natural lakes, he looks for deep holes on shallow flats. He has such an area on a small Michigan lake where he can catch 20 to 40 smallmouth a day in early spring.

"One end of the hole offers a steeper break, and it's adjacent to the flat where they spawn," he explains. "I think the steep break is the key to the smallmouth. While I might catch largemouth scattered around the hole, the smallies always are bunched in specific areas, and generally those are inside turns. If I've got wind blowing into that inside turn, it's even better."

Mangus thinks that wintering fish use those holes, and because it is on a shallow flat, that water warms first. Also, the fish have immediate access to shallow spawning grounds. He says that when the fish are active, they'll be as shallow as 7 feet,

but most of the time he catches them at about 10 feet. The bottom is relatively clean.

In the very early season, he likes 2-inch worms on light line and small jigheads. His favorite lure is a brown, 1/4- or 1/8-ounce hair jig with an Uncle Josh U-2 pork leech.

"Smallmouth seem to like the straight-tail better early, but as the water warms into the 50s, I'll fish the 3-inch Twister body on 1/8-ounce or 1/4-ounce jigheads," he explains. "The Twisters seem to work best when the fish are deeper. You have to experiment because their preference does seem to change, and I've seen it vary from one body of water to the other."

The Silver Buddy and other belly-weighted, metal vibrating baits also are effective on smallmouth during the early season. Mangus says the lure performs best over clean, hard bottoms when fish are actively feeding.

On reservoirs, as well as natural lakes, Mangus looks for deep water that swings close to the bank with slots and inside turns. A good example would be a point that drops into deep water and turns back toward shore.

"Smallmouth have a tendency to stack up around the inside turn of a point," he says. "That

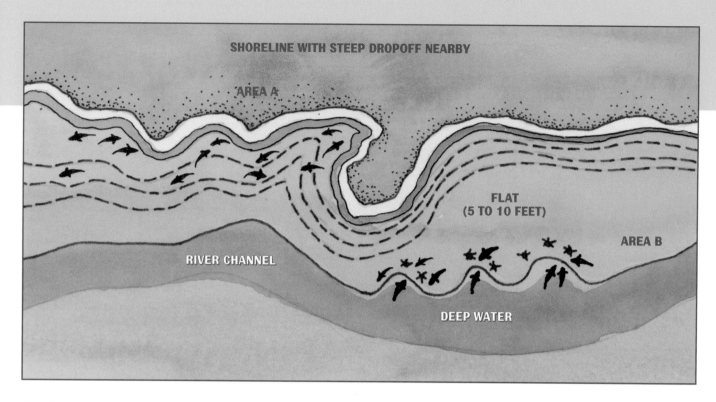

SHORELINE WITH STEEP DROPOFF NEARBY

AREA A

FLAT
(5 TO 10 FEET)

AREA B

RIVER CHANNEL

DEEP WATER

doesn't mean you won't find them elsewhere, but it's a good place to start the search."

On rivers and lakes with current, smallies are most active when the water is moving, and that's when he catches the bigger fish around rockpiles, slots off the main river channel or around bluff banks. If the current is too strong, they move closer to the banks, into the eddies where the water is slowed. Again, the jig-and-pork leech and Twister grubs are his top choices.

On Lake St. Clair — a drowned river mouth lake near Detroit — Michigan BASS pro Kim Stricker says smallmouth will stack up at the mouths of the numerous rivers and creeks that drop into the main lake. Those areas usually are found at the entrances of large bays filled with sandy, shallow bottoms and pencil reeds. Stricker says there are weedbeds at the river mouths, but they are scattered into isolated clumps.

"As the water begins to warm, the baitfish will stage there and the smallies aren't far behind," he says. "The weeds aren't fully developed and there are open pockets as they line the channel in 5 to 8 feet of water. The open lanes are where the current flows, and that's where I find the smallmouth."

Pearl-white Gitzits or white Twister grubs on 1/16-ounce jigheads are his favorite lures.

If the water warms into the 60s and fishing slows, Stricker knows to work into the bay, fishing spinnerbaits and Rat-L-Traps in and around the newly developed pencil reed.

"Not all of the fish move at the same time, and there always seem to be a few in the river mouth, but they do move shallower to spawn," he says. "They bed right at the base of the reeds in 2 to 5 feet of water. The better reeds are in small clumps. A chartreuse-and-white spinnerbait with a No. 5 willowleaf blade is ideal for that fishing."

The small number of anglers who fish for smallmouth in early spring perplexes Stricker.

And, as all the early spring anglers say, those wild smallmouth always put a charge into your heart when you need it most; after a long, hard winter.

INSIDE TURNS leading to spawning grounds are ideal. A depression on a flat (A) away from a main lake breakline is good. Slots off flats that tumble into deep water (B) produce during prespawn.

ALL SMALLMOUTH anglers need to keep a soft jerkbait readily available. Bronzebacks can't resist the darting action of the bait.

CATCHING A SMALLMOUTH of any size in the summer is an accomplishment. A lunker like this one is a prized possession.

SUMMERTIME SMALLMOUTH
Learn where bronzebacks stack up in warm weather

G O TO ANY LAKE THAT CONTAINS BOTH largemouth and smallmouth bass, and you can expect to find at least a few bigmouth hanging around cover in water 10 feet or less.

Smallmouth, on the other hand, are likely to be anywhere — except, of course, where you are fishing.

Inexplicably, the smallies that took the rod out of your hand during the spring seemingly vanish after the spawn. That's because they're ornery cusses, breaking all the rules that their largemouth cousins tend to follow.

"Smallmouth have developed their reputations for being difficult to catch through their unpredictable summertime habits," explains BASS pro Joe Thomas. "Perhaps that's why anglers hold them in such high esteem. When you catch a smallmouth, whatever its size, you feel a special sense of accomplishment."

As tough as smallmouth fishing can be during the summer, experts insist those rascals can be located and caught. It takes patience and an attitude adjustment.

"The first thing you've got to do is stop thinking 'largemouth' — and think 'smallmouth,' " says Hoosier Greg Mangus, a top smallmouth expert. "You have to differentiate between tactics and strategies for the two fish."

Most anglers assume smallmouth head deep once water temperatures rise into the high 70s, and rightfully so. But "deep" is a relative term. And the correct depth can vary from lake to lake.

"On most lakes, smallmouth will move to structure that's deeper than what bass fishermen like to fish," says Michigan pro Kevin VanDam. "That's no hard, fast rule, though. On shallow lakes, you can catch them consistently in 10 feet of water or less."

But those aren't typical of most smallmouth lakes. Generally, most prolific smallmouth waters have an abundance of deep water, which adds to angler woes. However, experts say that deep water mysteries can be solved if you follow some basic principles.

KEVIN VANDAM says smallmouth rarely swim downward to strike a lure presented horizontally. But they will swim upward to hit a bait moving overhead.

FOLLOW THE FORAGE

"Forage still dictates where the smallmouth go," insists

Rocky Topwater Tactics

■ **Type of lake** — Deep, clear glacial lake in the North.
■ **Features** — An abundance of rocky reefs and humps.
■ **Time of year** — Summer.
■ **Best pattern** — Work noisy topwater lures early and late in the day over boulders and large chunk rocks adjacent to main lake shoals. Water depth in these areas will average 10 feet, but there is great variation. In the morning, don't spend too long on one spot. Keep moving and casting, taking advantage of as much opportunity as possible until bright sunlight and boat traffic drive the fish down.
■ **Key to success** — Big rocks are a must for this pattern, since the water in this lake is clear, and smallmouth must have holes and shadows to hide in to ambush prey.

Shoal Bass

LARGE SHOALS offer a diversity of depth and structure. Use a jigging spoon as a search bait to cover water and find active smallmouth holding tight to the shoal.

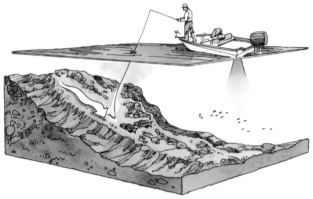

WHEN JOE THOMAS fishes ledges on the Great Lakes, he looks for depth where baitfish are holding to the nearest structure. He then positions the boat over deeper water and walks a grub down a dropoff.

Indiana bass guide Chip Harrison. "On Lake Wawasee near my home, smallmouth can be in two places at once: Some are up on the flats with the largemouth, feeding on crawfish, while the majority school over deep structure to feed on minnows.

"But on Torch Lake, an ultradeep lake in northern Michigan, summer smallmouth hang around the perch and alewives that are in deep water. On any lake, the key is to know what the primary forage is and monitor its movements. Find the bait and you'll find the smallmouth."

Locating deep water baitfish is easy if you've got good electronics. When smallmouth experts are looking for brownies, they idle over offshore structure, looking for balls of bait to appear on the fishfinder screen.

"You'll find a constant depth at which the bait is holding," explains Harrison. "Once you identify that depth, begin searching for the nearest structure."

For example, if he locates baitfish holding at 25 feet, he drives to the nearest bottom depth of 25 feet. That could be the end of a point, along a ledge or around a submerged island.

"The smallmouth suspending around open water baitfish aren't easy to catch, but those relating to the bottom or structure are catchable," he explains. "Sometimes I can see the fish on the screen and know they are smallmouth."

Thomas uses similar tactics when fishing for Lake Erie smallmouth during the summer, except he looks for the thermocline to help him identify their hideouts. Because oxygen and pH are inadequate below the thermocline, baitfish often stratify just above it. Once he identifies the depth pattern, he narrows the search to specific sections of the structure.

"I look for consistent baitfish readings on my Lowrance X-70 LCD," he describes. "Once I've determined the thermocline depth, I begin looking for structure that connects with that depth."

HOME IN ON STRUCTURE

"At that point, it becomes a simple matter of breaking down the structure," he describes. "In other words, look for the same key elements that you seek in shallow water structure — points, inside turns, a big boulder or two — any irregular features. Smallmouth will hold on those the same way largemouth use the shallow structure."

For deep, Great Lakes smallmouth, Thomas prefers to use 5-inch smoke or chartreuse metalflake grubs on quarter-ounce Darter jigheads and 8-pound-test MagnaThin line.

"I want to keep the grub on the edge of the breakline, hopping it down the dropoff the same way you would hop it down a flight of stairs," he explains. "You have to sit over deep water and pull the grub toward you; if you sit shallow and drag it up the dropoff, you're going to snag often or tear up your line in the jagged rocks along the bottom."

Boat control also is important, says Thomas. He watches his depthfinder closely, moving away from the structure if he sees the depth shrink, or toward the structure if the depth increases. When possible, he drops marker buoys on the key structure so he can maintain visual contact as well.

FISH OVER THEIR HEADS

VanDam says suspended smallmouth holding near deep structure can be caught by running lures over their heads.

"A few years ago, I won a Michigan BASS Federation tournament by fishing a (Bagley) DB3 crankbait in 25 feet of water off a long point," he recalls. "I ran the crankbait down the point, where it was touching bottom. I then continued to pull it through open water. Three- and 4-pound fish were coming up from 25 feet to smash the bait."

VanDam says he even tried fishing a Carolina rig, but the fish wouldn't touch it.

"That's something to remember about smallmouth," he offers. "They rarely go down to get a bait that is being presented horizontally, but they won't hesitate to go a long way up to get one moving overhead."

Those tactics work well on lakes with large, expansive flats where smallmouth hold on shallower structure. Bass will scatter over flats adjacent to deep water and can provide some fantastic action.

"That's especially true during windy days," VanDam adds. "It doesn't matter how clear the water is or how much cover is there. If you've got wind blowing across a lake that contains plenty of flats, you're going to catch smallies in 10 feet or less."

Chartreuse spinnerbaits, topwaters and lipless crankbaits are VanDam's favorites for fishing middepth flats. He says he's drawn hundreds of smallmouth strikes by fishing lures just beneath the surface in 10 to 15 feet of water.

"When fishing flats, the object is to keep moving, because the smallmouth can be anywhere," he explains. "You're looking for aggressive fish anyway, so those lures are going to be effective."

BE AN EARLY BIRD

All of the experts agree that smallmouth — regardless of whether they're deep or shallow — tend to be most active during low-light conditions. Thus, it's important to be on your best spot at first light.

"That's true for the shoal fish as well," says VanDam. "I don't think those fish migrate far, they simply move to the top of the shoal and feed more aggressively."

Thomas agrees. He says Lake Erie smallmouth move up the structure at night.

"I think smallmouth basically are nocturnal feeders, so first light is at the end of their peak feeding period," he describes. "The fish that move up are the most aggressive ones, so that's when you want to be fishing topwaters, crankbaits or spinnerbaits. But remember, they won't stray far from their primary deep structure."

SMALLMOUTH and grubs go hand-in-hand. Try using a twin-tail version on a leadhead for fish hanging in deep water.

AUTUMN SMALLMOUTH PATTERNS

Fall may be the most overlooked and least understood season

THE SUN THAT BLAZED just a few weeks earlier is lower and cooler on the fall horizon. Summer's sweltering days are gone, with autumn's low humidity more suited to man and beast. Hardwood forests have bright autumn colors. Northern-bred ducks and geese are massed and fidgety, tight clusters circling each dawn and dusk as nervous birds test their migratory wings.

Seasonal change is in the wind, and all wild creatures are preparing for winter. For smallmouth bass anglers, change is at hand, too.

Lakes and rivers that were jammed with boats and people are mostly vacant. School is back in session, and only on weekends are a few die-hard anglers out and about. Even some otherwise hard-charging bass fishermen take time out for

hunting seasons, leaving choice fall bronzeback fishing for the few who know where, when and how to catch some of the year's fattest, hardest fighting bass of all.

"Fall fish can be very aggressive, and we really hammer smallmouth in the 2- to 5-pound range, occasionally catching some weighing up to 7 pounds," says Dave Harbin, a longtime guide and angler on Tennessee's bronzeback-rich Pickwick Reservoir. "The very best places for fall smallmouth in lakes are main river channel edges, midlake bars, and points near dropoffs. The key spots are drops that go from 7 to 10 feet, down to 25 or 30 feet."

Some of the best bars are a mile long, he says, and he scores best by fishing them with a jig-and-pig or plastic worm. He says a Carolina rig also works well. His favorites for that rig are a 6-inch pumpkinseed lizard and a black lizard with yellow spots. A 4-inch craw worm also is great on a Carolina rig.

At times, autumn smallmouth are very active and readily hit crankbaits. Harbin says crawfish-colored models are best, and his favorites are No. 7 or 9 Rapala Shad Raps and Bagley DB3s. When smallmouth are holding deep, superdeep crankbaits like the Mann's Deep 20+ score for Harbin, too.

Veteran Iowa smallmouth bass angler Barry Day also is a believer in crankbaits for fall smallmouth. He generally fishes them slowly on 8-pound-test line, coaxing crankbaits down to 10 or 12 feet of water, and occasionally bumping bottom. He favors the Norman Deep Little N and the small Rapala Fat Rap. In windy weather, when jig fishing is impossible and casting crankbaits is tough, Day favors blade baits like the Silver Buddy and Bullet Bait.

Lure presentation and boat control are important to Day's successful autumn smallmouth catches.

"I like a little chop on the water, because when it's calm in fall and the water is clear, mature smallmouth are spooky," he contends. "When it's calm, and the fish are on rocky bars and points in only 8, 10 or 12 feet of water, you've got to make long casts, because boats and bronzebacks don't mix in fall. Sometimes it's best to anchor and work a hot spot, rather than 'bump' around an area.

"I like windy weather best, 10 to 15 miles per hour is good, and I've made my best fall catches during midday. When it's cold and smallmouth want a slower moving lure, I prefer small finesse worms over jigs, even the popular and time honored hair jigs. I haven't seen a situation in years when a no-action finesse worm hasn't worked just as well as a hair jig. And with built-in scents in some plastic worms, I think they can produce more strikes from reluctant smallmouth than even the best-tied, best-balanced hair jigs. Tube lures can be

Shoal Bass Magic

■ **Type of lake** — Deep, clear glacial lake in the North.
■ **Features** — An abundance of rocky reefs and humps.
■ **Time of year** — Fall.
■ **Best pattern** — Fishing this time of year in the North is hit-or-miss, depending on the weather. Fish a jig-and-pig for smallmouth along rocky shorelines and midlake shoals in 5 to 10 feet of water. Concentrate on rocks close to deep water. Make quartering casts into the bank, and work the bait back slowly through the rocks. As a backup plan, slow roll 1/2-ounce spinnerbaits just above the rocks.
■ **Key to success** — When one bank produces a couple of bites, continue working it. Smallmouth group up in late fall, and one short stretch of bank can produce several fish for patient anglers.

ROCKPILES along breaklines or dropoffs can be important contact areas for connecting with big schools of autumn smallmouth.

outstanding, too; my favorite is the Berkley Power Tube."

Location is the key to catching fall smallies, Harbin contends.

"Below dams, in backwater riprap areas, we catch *huge* smallmouth during October and November," he explains. "It's my favorite time for big smallmouth, and we get lots of 3-, 4-, and 5-pound fish tight to river riprap."

As water temperature cools in natural lakes and reservoirs, forage begins to vacate shallow water and move to deeper structure. Smallmouth follow the bait in bunches and can be very predictable in

their locations. Points with long, tapering gravel bars and deep water nearby hold smallmouth through the seasons. In autumn, the fish tend to live along sharp dropoffs or breaklines, which are easily located with a good depthfinder.

Offshore, submerged islands or humps also can be choice spots, with the deeper, steeper breaklines sometimes attracting the most smallmouth, especially as water temperatures decrease into the 60s and 50s. In shallow lakes where the water is only 40 feet deep or so, key breaklines to work may be only 15 to 25 feet down. In deeper waters with depths of 70 to 100 feet, choice breaklines may drop to 30 or 40 feet.

Humps can be so productive for autumn smallmouth that anglers can collect a good catch of bronzebacks simply by "running and gunning" humps through the course of a day.

Rock clusters or projections along breaklines or dropoffs can be important contact areas for locating big schools of autumn smallmouth. In some clear lakes, where weeds grow to depths of nearly 20 feet, sometimes locating a few green weedbeds in a lake that has mostly dead, brown weeds can be a haven for feeding smallmouth. Not many green weeds are needed to harbor minnows and other bass food, and when they are found on a deep hump or bar, plenty of fall bronzebacks may be nearby.

Some of North America's best autumn smallmouth bass fishing is found on sprawling Lake Erie, straddling the United States-Canada border. Smallmouth are fat and abundant, and fall fishing is tops. Bob Ceglarski, who has guided anglers for Lake Erie smallmouth for 25 years, says autumn bass on the big lake commonly are found on island structures, ledges and humps feeding on minnows tossed around by big waves and wind.

Ceglarski habitually uses bright-colored Lindy Fuzz-E-Grub jigs tipped with golden shiner minnows for Erie fall bass. He fishes them with a lift-and-drop retrieve, right along bottom near ledges while drifting. At times when smallmouth are reluctant to hit, he'll use softshell crawfish — filet mignon to a bronzeback. Sometimes he'll tip a Lindy jig with a whole crawfish, but usually he fishes the live bait with a simple No. 2 Mustad hook, which he barbs through the bait's back. He sinks the bait with a 1/4- to 1/2-ounce split shot, and allows the bait to crawl around bottom while keeping an open bail on his spinning outfit — the standard tackle he fishes with 6-pound-test line.

He says fall smallmouth commonly are schooled tight, and anglers are wise to cover a lot of water until a pod of fish is located — then they should use floating markers to pinpoint areas along structure where smallies are found.

"On a good fall day, when conditions are right, I've found enormous smallmouth schools fishing this way," he explains. "On many occasions, friends and I have marked a structure, anchored, and then caught 50 smallmouth — some weighing up to 4 pounds — before we moved the boat. That kind of smallmouth bass fishing *only* is available in fall!"

WHEN CHOOSING a crankbait for smallmouth bass, opt for one that imitates the fish's favorite meal — the crawfish.

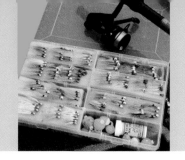

THE FLOAT-N-FLY
Try this hot bait for supercold smallmouth

EVERY ONCE IN A BLUE MOON, a system for bass comes along that's so unique, yet so refreshing in its simplicity, that it creates an instant sensation. You could *almost* say that about the Float-N-Fly, a lure technique used by east Tennessee smallmouth anglers that has gone mainstream in the bass fishing world.

This unusual system consists of a tiny minnowlike hair jig, a small plastic bobber, ridiculously light 4-pound line and the kind of rod that at first glance seems more at home in the steelhead rivers of the Pacific Northwest than the deep canyon lakes of Tennessee.

Bassmasters who have investigated the Float-N-Fly system know that it's the deadliest approach ever developed for midwinter smallies, short of live bait.

BIRTH OF THE FLOAT-N-FLY

The idea of suspending a tiny jig under a bobber isn't new — crappie fishermen have toyed it with for years. But you can credit the late Charlie Nuckols, an east Tennessee lure designer who created the modern Float-N-Fly system, for grasping the basic wisdom of the system, then refining it for smallmouth bass.

"When the water gets cold, and I'm talking way below 50 degrees, smallmouth often suspend in deep, clear lakes," Nuckols once recounted in *Bassmaster*. "When they do, they're extremely tough to catch on conventional lures and tackle. A jig or crankbait might run past them, but it's in and out of the strike zone before you can whistle Dixie."

AVOID USING fluorescent lines when fishing a Float-N-Fly. Clear mono will increase your catch rate significantly, especially on sunny days.

Smallies suspending in frigid water are anything but aggressive, Nuckols emphasized. "They won't chase a lure far. You've got to drop it right in front of their noses and keep it there if you want a bite."

Flies For Frigid Water

■ **Type of lake** — Highland reservoir in the upper South.
■ **Features** — Deep, rocky structure with little cover.
■ **Time of year** — Winter.
■ **Best pattern** — The first bitter cold spell of winter typically stuns smallmouth bass and causes them to move off the banks and suspend. Find their depth with sonar and set the fly that far beneath the bobber. Shake the rod tip as you slowly retrieve the rig, pausing occasionally to let the tiny jig sink. Keep the boat 20 to 40 yards away from the bank, and try a variety of locations until you can put a pattern together.
■ **Key to success** — Float-N-Fly fishing works well in clear water anytime water temperatures are in the mid-50s and colder. Fishing is best in the nastiest weather.

Enter the Float-N-Fly — the quintessential cold water presentation. "About 10 years ago, I started playing around with a tiny crappie jig rigged under a bobber," Nuckols recalled. "I figured a smallmouth in frigid water might hit something real small dangled right in its face."

Sure enough, Nuckols caught some bass on it, but he wasn't totally satisfied. The flies (hair jigs) he was using were crudely tied and didn't look very realistic in the extremely clear water of the east Tennessee lakes he frequented. And the only floats he was able to find were way too big and clunky.

Nuckols began tying his own jigs. He experimented with several materials and patterns, making a mental note of how the bass responded to each. He refined his presentation techniques until he could consistently catch smallmouth in water below 40 degrees. Soon, he was picking the pockets of other area smallmouth nuts in weekend winter pot tournaments as well. And the Float-N-Fly system was born.

The Float-N-Fly technique is now standard procedure on many smallmouth and spotted bass lakes in cold weather.

NEW DIRECTIONS

One of the most enthusiastic advocates of the Float-N-Fly system is Tennessee smallmouth fanatic Tom Orr. He has caught over 20 smallmouth a day using the Float-N-Fly on several occasions at

Casting The Float-N-Fly

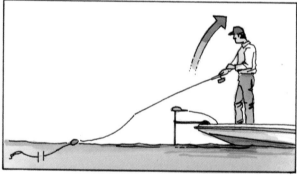

1 — Stand up and face your target, with the rod pointed ahead and the Float-N-Fly in the water ahead of you.

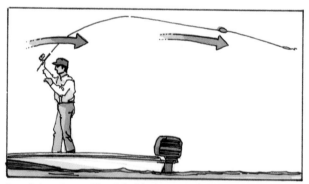

2 — Bring the rod back behind you and wait for the lure to stretch out behind, as in fly casting.

3 — Cast lure to the target and wait for the fly to sink.

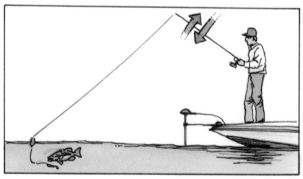

4 — Gently shake the rod to activate the fly. Pause, reel one or two turns and repeat. The float will disappear or lean over when a fish strikes.

Dale Hollow, Center Hill and other classic middle Tennessee smallmouth impoundments, even with water temperatures only in the upper 30s. And just because the fly is tiny, don't get the mistaken impression that it catches only small fish. "My biggest smallmouth so far on the Float-N-Fly is just over 5 pounds. Surprisingly, you don't catch many undersized bass on it — unlike other finesse methods, the Float-N-Fly is a big fish system."

There's a saying that you can't have too much fun, and that quickly became Tom Orr's philosophy with this unorthodox method. "Without a doubt, Float-N-Fly fishing is the most fun fishing there is. It's like bluegill fishing when you were a kid, only multiplied to the 100th power."

The Float-N-Fly has now gained so much widespread popularity that anglers like Orr use it year-round. But winter remains the best time to use the technique, according to Orr.

"It is the most dependable time to catch fish on the Float-N-Fly, because it's the perfect lure and presentation for inactive, suspending bass," according to Orr, whose tackle system is adjusted according to the conditions.

"I start with a 1/16-ounce fly 8 1/2 to 9 feet below the bobber and target main lake points and bluffs. If I'm not getting any action, I assume the bass are deeper, and will raise the float to 11 or 12 feet from the jig. At those depths I may switch to a 1/8-ounce fly and a slightly larger bobber for easier casting. I'll begin at daybreak fishing a pale gray jig with just a touch of chartreuse in it. As the sun comes up, I'll switch to silver or gray with a bit of pink. Your best luck will always be on shady banks or on overcast days. A light chop helps."

THE "FLY" PART of the rig is not all-important — any little crappie jig will do. The commotion created by the bobber on top of the water is what generates the attention of bass.

More Float-N-Fly Tips

As you learn to fish the Float-N-Fly, practice these tips the pros recommend.

■ Don't overwork the Float-N-Fly, especially in cold water. Sometimes "deadsticking" the float and letting it bob gently in choppy water is the best approach.

■ Try tipping the fly with various trailers. Tennessee smallmouth expert Tom Orr has had good results by adding a tiny Berkley Power Bait soft plastic crappie maggot or a live tuffy minnow to the hook.

■ Keep a sharp eye on the bobber. If it leans over sideways, your fly is either on the bottom or you've got a fish.

■ In murky lakes, increase the intensity of the fly's color. Chartreuse and hot pink work best in low-visibility conditions.

■ Avoid fluorescent lines. Clear mono can increase your catch rate dramatically, especially on sunny days.

■ Not every bite you'll get on the Float-N-Fly will be from a smallmouth bass. Spotted bass love the tiny flies, as do trout, crappie, white bass, hybrids, even

stripers. You'll catch fewer largemouth on it, however.

■ Even though a quality spinning reel is imperative, don't rely on the drag system when battling a big smallmouth. Most experienced Float-N-Fly anglers switch off the reel's antireverse, preferring to back-reel instead of trusting drag systems.

■ Break off above the bobber and rerig after catching a quality fish. Most line abrasion occurs when the light mono is stretched against the metal clip of the bobber during a bass' struggles.

BASS WATERS

To fully understand bass behavior,
you must first understand
its environs …

PRESENT LURES into any irregularities in slop, especially where the growth forms points, indentations or holes.

FIVE CAN'T-MISS PATTERNS FOR NATURAL LAKES

Try these surefire hot spots for bass

IF YOU CAN COUNT to five, you can pattern bass on natural lakes.

Anglers who fish those divine bodies of water located throughout most Northern states (and Southern states as well) say that one or more of five basic patterns will produce bass even on the toughest days.

Natural lakes are different from reservoirs be-

cause they are void of dams, flooded timber, creek channels, river ledges and stumpfields. Also, they don't fluctuate or change water clarity as often. Because of the lack of structure, the fish have fewer options in where they live and feed.

"Although it may be easier to locate quantities of bass on a reservoir, you only have five primary patterns to check on natural lakes," says BASS pro

Kevin VanDam. "And it doesn't take long to figure out which ones are the most productive."

Those patterns — channels, docks, inside weed edges, outside dropoffs and "slop" — attract the largest percentage of bass on most natural lakes. You can count on at least one of those patterns producing fish.

Here's a look at each pattern, and tips on how to fish it efficiently:

1. INSIDE WEED EDGES

When bass on the main lake aren't deep or holding tight to the shore, chances are they can be caught from middepth waters between the shore and the first major dropoff.

"That's always the first place I start," says Chip Harrison, who guides on Indiana lakes in the summer and on Florida's Lake Okeechobee during winter. "I always presume the fish will be on the inside edge of every lake I fish. You can usually catch some fish deep, but they aren't as easy to catch as those using the inside edge."

Harrison says the inside edge differs from lake to lake. On some lakes, the inside edge is closer to shore, while on others, the weed edge may be on the outer edge of vast flats, close to the first major dropoff.

While Harrison agrees that the flats on the inside edge aren't as productive during cold front conditions, he doesn't believe the fish move far away. If anything, he says, they simply draw tighter to the weed edges, and their strike zones shrink.

"You have to slow down and fish the edge of the vegetation more thoroughly," he explains.

"Key on the edges with the points and cuts that extend toward shallower water. The fish use those irregular features just like they do other types of cover and structure."

On Northern lakes, he prefers to scoot natural-colored Yamamoto grubs along the bottom near the weed edges. If the fish are aggressive, he switches to a spinnerbait, lipless crankbait or topwater, like a Pop-R. In Florida's natural lakes, bass seem to prefer larger baits that can be fished faster, such as spoons, lipless crankbaits, spinnerbaits and 10-inch worms.

2. OUTSIDE WEED EDGES

The deeper edge of weedline dropoffs is the best place to catch good numbers of quality bass, insists LaPorte, Ind., expert Mike Czanderna.

"A lot of people fish the outside edge, but most don't fish where the big ones live," he explains. "The bigger fish hold in that transition zone in slightly deeper water where the weeds stop growing."

Czanderna, who probably has caught more bass over 5 pounds than any other northern Indiana angler, believes big bass sit outside the weeds and watch for forage that wanders away from the thicker weeds.

Flipping For Grass Bass

■ **Type of lake** — Natural lake in the Midwest.

■ **Features** — Aquatic vegetation holds both largemouth and smallmouth bass.

■ **Time of year** — Summer.

■ **Best pattern** — Fantastic summer action can be found by flipping milfoil beds with a 1/2- to 3/4-ounce jig-and-craw or Texas rigged worm. Concentrate on working odd features — holes, indentations, points, isolated milfoil clumps, etc. — in 12 to 17 feet of water. Cover plenty of water in search of tight schools of bass. Also, clear days are better than cloudy ones, since the sunshine concentrates the fish in cover.

■ **Key to success** — Pay close attention to the specifics about the cover where your first bass comes from, then try to duplicate those conditions in other areas.

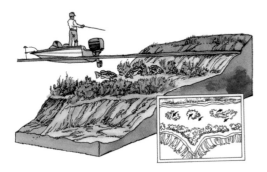

PROBE THE SHALLOW edge of vegetation between the shoreline and a dropoff when fishing inside weed edges.

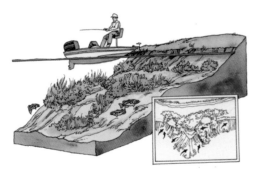

KEY ON SPARSE grass growing near a primary weedline when fishing the outside edge of vegetation.

BASS MOVE INTO slop during cold fronts and when nearby flats receive heavy fishing pressure.

CANALS ARE BASS magnets in spring and summer. Key spots include docks, vegetation and brushpiles. Also try the center of the channel and the first dropoff near the mouth during cold fronts.

DOCKS ARE BEST on cloudy days because fish are more aggressive and less likely to see the angler.

That's why he says boat positioning is so critical. He uses his depthfinder to ensure he's sitting away from the weeds, and casts toward the weed edge. He maneuvers the boat slowly and methodically into the wind, so that he doesn't miss a subtle change in the structure that could hold a school of big bass. Also, he pays close attention to what his lure tells him.

He prefers to fish deep running crankbaits along the outside edge, but sometimes thick weeds prohibit a good presentation. Under those conditions, he fishes a large jig tipped with either a plastic crawfish or a pork trailer.

3. SLOP FISHING

When you suspect bass are using the heavy cover, head for the lily pads and floating debris that gather in backwater shallows.

"When conditions push bass to the heavy cover, fish that cruise nearby flats will stack up in these areas," says Michigan BASS pro Kim Stricker. "They're not always easy to catch, but when you do hook up, it's usually a good fish."

Unless he knows the fish have pulled into the interior of the slop, Stricker targets the outside edge first, throwing at points and pockets. If there's another edge closer to shore, he'll work it, too.

"Most people won't go to the trouble of fishing the inside edge, but it can be worthwhile," he explains. "That's what you've got to remember about slop fishing: The harder it is to do, the more likely you'll encounter fish that haven't seen many lures."

Stricker likes weedless spoons, weedless surface lures and floating worms for the thick stuff. If the pads are floating on the surface, his favorite is a Herb's Dilly, a bladed lure (similar to a buzzbait) that sputters on the surface.

4. CHANNELS

On many natural lakes, canals have been dug to connect other lakes or waterfront residential areas to the main body of water. Because these man-made canals are protected from the wind and are relatively shallow, they warm up quickly and attract large schools of prespawn and spawning bass.

Channel banks may offer the best shallow water habitat, but VanDam says anglers shouldn't overlook the deeper areas.

"Fishing pressure or cold fronts will push canal bass off the shoreline and into the deeper, center section of the channel," he adds. "If the channels are getting a lot of pressure, fish a jig-and-pork slowly down the middle. Inactive fish don't leave the channels, they just slide to the middle and hug the bottom."

Also, most canals are connected to the lake by a shallow flat that drops abruptly at the channel mouth. That subtle ledge often serves as a staging area for bass moving in and out of the channel.

"Those cuts with 6 feet of water or more hold fish year-round," VanDam has found. "I've fished channels where I could almost guarantee a fish from a specific spot, and catch that same fish three or four times a year. That's how territorial they can be."

That doesn't mean channel fish can be easy to catch during the summer season. VanDam says they can be tough to fool because of the fishing pressure they get from shore anglers who live around the channel. That's why he eases into channels quietly and takes the time to line up his casts perfectly for the best presentation.

5. DOCKS

Like channels, boat docks can be productive from early spring through late fall.

"Docks serve the same purpose as shoreline logs and stumps you find in rivers and reservoirs," says Indiana pro Ken McIntosh. "Even though the water is crystal clear and the bottom clean, bass will hold under docks from spring through fall."

McIntosh agrees with anglers who say the dock pattern is good on bright days, but he still prefers to fish them under cloudy skies.

"The overcast pulls the fish shallow, and the dock provides the cover for an ambush area," he explains. "The fish tend to be more aggressive around docks on cloudy days."

Any dock can hold fish, says McIntosh, but single piers on an open stretch of shoreline are surefire winners. He also concentrates on docks positioned on the back side of shallow flats — docks most anglers ignore.

Docks don't have to have an abundance of cover beneath them, either. McIntosh prefers docks with no vegetation around them because the fish see his lures better.

"The fish suspend under boats and in the shady areas where you can't see them," he explains. "That's when it's important to get your lures far under the pier and not just around the perimeter."

When the water is cold or he suspects schooling bass are roaming the shorelines, he opts for skipping soft plastic baits under piers with spinning gear. But during dog days, when large bass move into pier structures, he goes to a big jig and a flipping rod.

"I'm fishing for one big bite," he explains. "I'll fish with the wind to my back, using it to help move me along the shore rather than bumping the trolling motor button, which I believe can spook fish around piers."

SKIP SOFT PLASTIC baits under piers when schooling bass are roaming the shoreline.

USE A BUZZBAIT parallel to the edges of grass for explosive topwater strikes.

TIPS FOR AGING RESERVOIRS

Find new life in old lakes with these tips

BASS HABITS AND HABITATS can change drastically as a reservoir ages. Knowing how to adapt to their ongoing aging process is a key to finding success on dated impoundments.

Dan Morehead, who grew up fishing famed Kentucky Lake, has a knack for patterning fish on these timeless fisheries. Created in 1944, Kentucky Lake is still a top producer for anglers like Morehead who can tap into the potential of such timeless fisheries.

CHANGING TIMES

Morehead listed some of the changes that typically occur as a reservoir ages:

• *Disappearing wood* — "Submerged brush and spindly trees disappear quickly, especially in shallow water," he says. "They're broken up by current and wave action. This stuff is great shallow bass cover, and it also provides a sanctuary for baitfish and bass fry. When it starts disappearing, many bass will move to offshore structure and the shallow bite will suffer dramatically. Also, exposed standing timber lining creek channels eventually topples over and rots away."

• *Contours soften* — "Over time, the reservoir's structural features become less well-defined; again, this happens first in shallow water. Ditches and shallow creek channels fill in with silt. Humps, bars, even roadbeds are smoothed out by wave action and current."

• *Cover is repositioned* — "During flooding, rising water picks up shoreline wood and may uproot entire trees. This wood is carried by current down the reservoir system and may end up at the head of an island, on a flat or bar, etc., where little or no cover had existed before."

WHEN SHORELINE cover has all but disappeared, bass will relate to nearby points or ledges, where they suspend when inactive.

• *Cover is introduced* — "Where legal, many fishermen sink brushpiles in the reservoir to attract gamefish, especially crappie. This also lures bass back into the shallows."

• *Weed explosion* — "So-called 'junk weeds,' like milfoil and hydrilla, can enter the reservoir system where little or no submerged grass existed before. On Kentucky Lake, fishing was tough for several years once the shallow brush disappeared. Then milfoil made its way into the reservoir via the Tombigbee Waterway. The weed cover spread throughout the reservoir like wildfire, and in about three years the lake's bass productivity skyrocketed."

• *Disappearing vegetation* — "The reverse can be true — as some reservoirs age, vegetation can disappear. Newly inundated shoreline grasses die and rot

away quickly. Herbicides, grass carp and other methods may be employed to kill widespread weeds. Aquatic plants produce oxygen, filter the water to make it cleaner, and provide great bass habitat. When weeds disappear, fishing inevitably suffers."

• *Erosion* — "The shoreline may be gradually eaten away by current and wave action from barges and pleasure boats. This can impact shallow bass patterns dramatically. I know three islands on Kentucky Lake that were once as big as football fields and have now almost totally disappeared due to erosion. All that mud and silt has to go somewhere, so it washes into the system and ends up 'softening' structural contours. Erosion can sometimes change fishing for the better. If the bank erodes and shoreline trees topple into the water,

A Slow Roll For Prespawners

■ **Type of lake** — Large mainstream reservoir in the South.

■ **Features** — Aquatic vegetation is replacing dense stands of flooded timber as the primary cover.

■ **Time of year** — Late winter.

■ **Best pattern** — After a series of warm days signals the approach of spring, follow the bass into shallow pockets, near where spawning will eventually take place. Any cover in those pockets will concentrate prespawn bass, which can be caught by slow rolling a 1/2-ounce spinnerbait over and through logs, stumps and weeds. Best spots will be where a channel or ditch swings close to the bank, offering quick access to deep water.

■ **Key to success** — Fish the warm part of the day. Afternoons are usually best, after the water temperature warms through the morning.

new bass cover is created. On Kentucky Lake, eroding mud has revealed gravel and rock that serve as prime smallmouth habitat; I've caught smallies weighing over 7 pounds here in recent years where I'd seldom catch any before."

• *Water clarity changes* — "Many reservoirs become clearer over time as silt settles and the nutrient level of the water diminishes."

• *Water quality changes* — "A reservoir may see an increase or decrease in water quality over time. Nationwide, many impoundments have better water quality than they did years ago. But impoundments with extensive shoreline development can suffer declining water quality."

SHIFTING DEEPER

When shallow wood cover has disappeared in an aging reservoir, Morehead looks for bass in deeper water. "I've found that deeper patterns aren't nearly as susceptible to change as are shallow patterns in an older lake," he informs. "The shoreline and adjacent shallow bass cover gets hammered by wave or current action, rising and falling water, etc. Deeper cover isn't pounded by waves so much and is never exposed to direct sunlight, so it rots slowly. Deep stumps and tree limbs may 'petrify' and become hard as rocks."

Bass are far more attuned to offshore structure in aging impoundments, Morehead has found. "In some older reservoirs, the banks are virtually slick, so there's really no reason for the bass to be shallow. They gravitate instead to main lake points, humps, creek and river channel dropoffs, etc. Here, their feeding opportunities are greatest; bass often hold on these structures and wait for baitfish schools to pass by."

Deeper structure can be more difficult to locate as time passes, the pro has learned; this can be especially frustrating when using a topo map. "Most contour maps were made when the reservoir was young, so the structure you're trying to find may not even be there now," Morehead warns. "If you're having trouble matching your topo map to reality, check the date on the back."

When you do locate deeper cover or structure, use marker buoys to delineate your target, Morehead suggested. "Most of these deeper bass spots are well off the banks, so it's harder to stay oriented to them. Buoys give you a visible target. Also, I've found a GPS unit is especially handy in an older impoundment, for it can put you back on these deeper offshore spots quickly."

Bass often suspend more in an older reservoir, Morehead adds. "Although most of the lake's bass were tight to shallow cover when the impoundment was young, they'll gradually move off the banks as this habitat disappears. They'll cruise down a

DAN MOREHEAD believes in using obscure tactics for jaded bass in aging impoundments. This fish was caught by bouncing a bucktail jig on a deep hump.

How Reservoirs Age

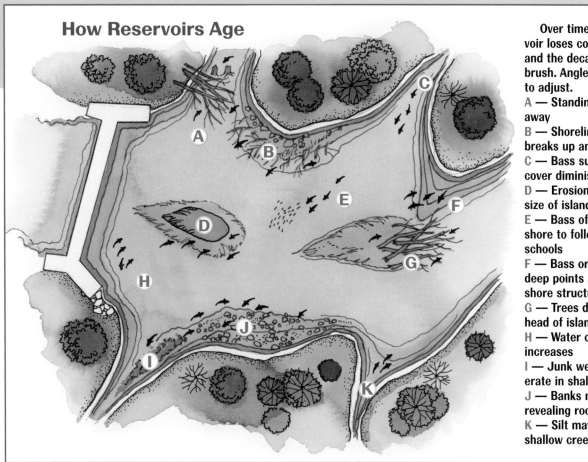

Over time, every reservoir loses cover to siltation and the decay of trees and brush. Anglers must learn to adjust.

A — Standing timber rots away

B — Shoreline brush breaks up and rots away

C — Bass suspend more as cover diminishes

D — Erosion may reduce size of islands

E — Bass often move offshore to follow baitfish schools

F — Bass orient more to deep points and other offshore structure

G — Trees deposited at head of island during flood

H — Water clarity often increases

I — Junk weeds may proliferate in shallow water

J — Banks may erode, revealing rock or gravel

K — Silt may close off shallow creek arms

point, ledge or hump and suspend over it when they aren't actively feeding. In winter, bass often move to deep tributary arms and suspend around clouds of shad — there's nothing holding them there except the bait."

FISHING POINTERS

Fishing an older reservoir often requires a vastly different approach than was needed when the lake was new, Morehead insists. "The most critical thing to remember is that shallow shoreline patterns often go sour as the impoundment gets older. If you've fished the lake since it was young, you'll remember when the shallow fishing was great. This may keep you going back to the shallows year after year, even after the fishing there has declined. If you'll move out to the first significant depth change, you'll often contact bass. Look especially for isolated cover in deeper water."

A Carolina rigged worm or lizard and a deep diving crankbait are highly recommended by Morehead for probing aging impoundments. These lures cover a lot of water quickly and are ef-

fective for hugging deep contours, he says.

Morehead has found downsizing often pays off big in an old reservoir. "Often the water has gotten clearer and the fish more wary. Bass under these conditions always bite better when you use smaller lures and lighter line. You may have to buy a couple of spinning outfits as your home reservoir gets older."

Finally, Morehead stresses the importance of being creative in your fishing approach when you're facing the challenge of patterning an old-timer reservoir. "I can't tell you how many times I've gotten on fish quickly by doing something off-the-wall, like fishing a heavy bucktail jig in deep water when other anglers were using a crankbait. Fish get used to the same old lures and presentations over time, and throwing 'em a change-up can turn the tide in your favor."

IF YOUR "GO-TO" bait isn't producing in an area that you know holds bass, downsize.

DAVY HITE, a master of hydroelectric river-run impoundments, has found that pulling water moves bait to key ambush areas around bass structure.

RIVER WAYS:
THE CURRENT AFFAIRS
Finding bass on rivers can be surprisingly simple

THE ALLURE OF BIG WATER and anglers' ever-increasing infatuation with sophisticated fishing techniques have pulled many people away from their bassing wellsprings: the rivers of America. One result of that separation is that many anglers forget the fundamentals they figured out by trial and error as youngsters along the stream banks.

Rivers, naturally, remain prime places for all bass species. In fact, largemouth, smallmouth, spotted bass and their lesser-known cousins cruised the currents long before the valleys were straddled by giant dams that backed the waters up into the countryside's farms, meadows and woodlands.

While there are scores of differences between

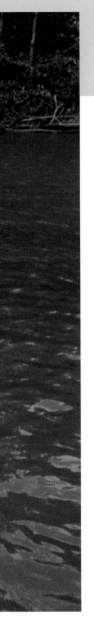

rivers and lakes, the biggest variable is also the most obvious: current.

"Fish always position themselves according to the current in a river," says Joe Thomas, a BASS touring pro from the Cincinnati, Ohio, area. Thomas matured as a bass fisherman working the fickle Ohio River.

Another Ohio River veteran is Gary Brown, who says river fishing is simply a matter of following the seasonal patterns. "It's simpler, for me, on rivers than on the reservoirs, where you have a lot more variables," Brown says.

Many pro anglers point to Woo Daves of Spring Grove, Va., as one of the finest river anglers in the United States. Daves has proved his expertise as a riverman with victories on some of America's toughest waterways, including the Mississippi River.

"Ninety-five percent of bass caught in rivers come from 4 feet of water or less," he says. "They don't want to fight the main currents, so they tend to stay up shallow where they can find a lot of things to break the flow; things like stumps, logs, docks, pilings and even trash that washes into eddy pockets."

LOCATING RIVER BASS

The three experts agree that once anglers locate river bass, the fish tend to be relatively easy to catch. But where does the search begin?

For Brown, the first choices usually are the feeder creeks.

"In spring, I go to the backs of the creeks, as far back as they go, and start working likely looking places," he explains. "In spring and fall, this creek location really isn't that much different than where you might start on a reservoir."

Daves, meanwhile, uses his shallow water tactics on rivers across the United States.

"The only time, usually, that you might catch fish deeper than 4 or 5 feet is on rivers that don't have much current, like the Arkansas River, with all its (navigation) locks."

Thomas says anglers can expect to encounter different species as they move about on a specific stretch of river. As more and more rivers, including his Ohio River, came to be tamed by locks and dams, the bass found their preferred locations.

Smallmouth, in general, settle in around the upper stretches of pools, where the water often is clearer and the current swifter after pouring over or through the dams. To find smallies, Thomas scouts the main channel side of the river, looking specifically for places with chunk rocks or broken-shale banks. Then, he zeroes in further by casting toward the current breaks in those upstream locations.

Thomas notes that largemouth and spotted bass might come from those locations, but they are more likely to prefer the downstream places where the current isn't as powerful. Largemouth, in particular, will move into the weedbeds.

Fish Ledges In The Flow

■ **Type of lake** — River-run reservoir in the mid-South.
■ **Features** — Extensive flooded buckbrush, stumpfields and occasional patches of vegetation.
■ **Time of year** — Summer.
■ **Best pattern** — In rivers as well as river-run reservoirs, summer bass concentrate along deep ledges. Look for river/creek channel junctions, underwater humps, roadbeds and other structure in water that drops from 12 feet into 25 or 30 feet. Work these spots with shad-colored crankbaits that run at least as deep as the top of the ledge. Excellent backup lures are jigs and Carolina rigged lizards.
■ **Key to success** — The best time to fish this pattern is when current is running. Current moves baitfish and triggers a feeding period for bass. When the current kicks on, get to your best spot.

BASS WILL HOLD in current breaks created by laydowns or other wood structure.

LOCATIONS WITHIN LOCATIONS

Once a fisherman is within sniffing distance of bass, the places into which he dunks his lures are critical. That is, once the general location pattern is identified, the angler must further eliminate options by knowing where along the bank the fish are stationed.

The first choice, and most obvious, is the best one: current breaks.

"I always stop and fish sand and gravel bars on the downriver side of feeder creeks," Thomas says. "The downstream side of a bar is consistently good because it creates an eddy in the current and attracts baitfish."

Daves, a self-proclaimed "junk" fisherman, applies his hunt-and-peck style on rivers. "I look for bass behind anything that breaks the flow: rockpiles, pier pilings, logs, brush, stuff like that."

Bass hold behind the current breaks with their noses pointing into the flow. This allows them to maintain control over their bodies, just as it's easier for an angler to control the position of his boat if the bow and trolling motor are pointing right into the current.

The current direction dictates the bass' position even more than the sun and shadows, although a bass often can find a compromise that allows it to settle into a shaded current break.

TRIGGERING THE STRIKE

Once the angler is in the right place on the river and positioned to hit the most likely looking spots, the hard work is over, according to Brown. Worms, jigs and spinnerbaits, with topwater lures

as conditions merit, will get the job done.

"This is where people who are more experienced on reservoirs sometimes have trouble on the rivers," he says. "Basically, if they'll remember to downsize their lures from what they use on the lakes, they'll be better off."

In spring, when the water temperature is still in the mid to upper 40s, Brown starts with a 1/8-ounce jig trimmed with an Uncle Josh U2 pork. As the water warms, he mixes pitching the jig with slinging spinnerbaits. His choices are 1/8- to 1/4-ounce spinnerbaits with tandem blades: No. 1 or 2 trailed by a No. 3 or 4.

Brown's summer tactics include pitching a worm or Super Do (a soft plastic crawfish) into the pockets and points along the outside edge of grasslines. He also works the tops of the weeds with buzzbaits and the Basswater Popper, a hollow latex lure with a concave face. And lately he's found a merthiolate Zoom floating worm to be effective on river-weed bass.

Fall finds Brown back in the creeks with his spinnerbaits and Super Dos.

CURRENT IS the key to turning on fish in hydroelectric fisheries.

WHEN CURRENT IS present on an impoundment, target offshore structure where bass will suspend as they ambush prey pulled by the current.

Thomas, like others who make their living on the professional bass trail, prefers to cover water quickly and efficiently. That often calls for crankbait tactics.

"My favorite way to catch river bass — shallow or medium depths — is with a 1/4-ounce chrome Bass Magnet," he says.

For the smallmouth Thomas occasionally targets in the upper stretches of river pools, he offers up an assortment that includes buzzbaits, the chrome Bass Magnet and the tried-and-true ballhead jig with a grub.

Lure choice is equally simple for Woo Daves, who stocks his box with small lures. His river kit includes 4 1/2-inch Woo Worms by Mr. Twister, 1/8- and 1/4-ounce spinnerbaits and a few crankbaits, including the Bagley Kill'r B1, the firetiger Model A Bomber and Rat-L-Traps.

"On rivers with small shad, like the Mississippi, Tennessee and a few others, I even use a Mepps spinner, the in-line model with squirrel tail on the hook," Daves says. "I've caught the big bass several times on it during tournaments on the James River."

River ways. Simple, really, reminding one of the days when fishing wasn't yet a high-tech sport. The days when a young angler took a single rod and a cherished lure to the local riverbank and cast out in hopes of catching a bragging-size bass to show off to buddies. The days when going fishing meant coming home with muddy sneakers. The time when bassing was a simple pursuit.

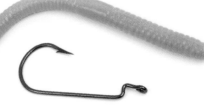

A FLOATING WORM is a great option for the slackwater areas in rivers. The spasmodic action of the bait imitates easy prey for current dwelling bass.

When dams are placed along a river system, the character of the impoundments created changes with the terrain, the wealth or scarcity of backwater areas, and the amount of cover or structure. Current flow also varies from place to place, but still retains its pivotal role in angling success.

Although bass fishermen have become rather adept at evaluating natural phenomena and adjusting to such changes, when it comes to the current, none of those talents can help in river impoundments. It's not that fishermen have trouble assessing the effects of current flow, because it's a basic, accepted fact that when the water is moving, fishing gets better.

The problem is simple: The human entity responsible for the water and the pace at which it is pulled (removed) from the impoundment doesn't follow any predictable schedule. As a result, the whole process of determining when, how and where to fish becomes a guessing game.

"On a hydroelectric lake, you have absolutely no control. You're at the mercy of the guy pulling the water," observes BASS pro Davy Hite, recognized by his peers as a master of fishing hydroelectric river impoundments.

In conditioning the fish, pulling water moves bait to key ambush areas around cover or structure. The bass quickly learn that moving water means prime feeding opportunities, and they become conditioned to feed at these prime times. When the water stops flowing, it stops pulling bait to these ambush points, and the fish tend to suspend. Also, they get programmed not to feed as much during nongeneration periods, when the water isn't moving.

"If they're pulling water and the water level is falling, you need to fish offshore structure. If they're not pulling water, you need to do something instead of just waiting for the water to move. You need to think about moving shallow or changing your techniques," concludes Hite.

ON THE falling tide, bass stage on the first dropoff nearby to feed on bait swept their way.

HOW TO CATCH TIDEWATER BASS

Some of America's best bassing is found in tidal zones

THROUGHOUT LARGE AREAS of coastal America, there are rivers, creeks and bayous close enough to salt water to be tidal in nature. As marine tides ebb and flood, so do adjacent freshwater bodies. For bass anglers more familiar with lakes and rivers far from the sea, tidal waters are an interesting challenge — and a rich opportunity!

The first challenge is that tidal waters are ever-changing. For example, a grass flat in a river 30 miles from the ocean may give up plenty of bass one morning, but by midafternoon not only have the bass disappeared, but the river actually is flowing in the opposite direction.

The submerged hump you caught a 5-pounder from today at noon may be an island tomorrow at dawn. And the creek mouth that had schooling bass and current pouring out of it today, could have water flooding into it next week at the same time of day, with no bass to be seen.

Tide is the rise and fall of water caused by the moon's gravitational effect on the earth. Tide causes current, which by definition is the lateral flow of water. A rising tide in the ocean pushes against river water flowing in at the coast. Ocean tides are so strong, they can "back up" the largest rivers to such an extent that freshwater rivers actually reverse their current flows for well over 100 miles from the ocean mouth — at least until the tide ebbs or falls.

Tide strength varies from one day to the next and is affected to some extent by wind and other environmental factors. What is more, in some regions there are two tides per day — meaning two high tides, two low tides in 24 hours.

In other areas — most notably along the Gulf

Slack Off On Winter Bass

■ **Type of lake** — Tidal river in the East.
■ **Features** — Abundant weedbeds in warm weather; some rocks.
■ **Time of year** — Winter.
■ **Best pattern** — Cold temperatures and moving water pose difficult fishing conditions, but you can eliminate one of those negatives in tidal

rivers by fishing at times when tides are slack. Look for pockets and deep holes where water isn't moving, and time your visit to the dead tide periods. Use smaller lures, including jig-and-pigs and grubs, that you can fish slowly. Lipless crankbaits and spinnerbaits also work when bass are more aggressive.
■ **Key to success** — When the tidal current does kick in, move 8 or 10 miles up or down the river to where the tide isn't moving.

MANY TIDAL rivers
have sharply defined
ledges, which are pre-
mier bass holding
structure.

of Mexico — there is just one tide per day. In some locales, tides are barely noticeable, changing water depth just a few inches, while in other places tide levels may exceed 10 feet! Moreover, the timing of tides varies from one day to the next. High tide today may be at noon, while tomorrow it's at 12:50 p.m., and the next day, 1:40 p.m.

This no doubt sounds confusing and not particularly fun for fishing to some bass anglers unfamiliar with tidewater. But, thankfully, tides and resulting currents are reasonably predictable, with tide charts readily available in coastal fishing areas from marinas, tackle shops and in regional daily newspapers. This predictability, and the fact that not all high tides or low tides occur at the same time in different places in a given region, make for outstanding bass action for seasoned anglers who know the tidewater score.

"There is a good degree of consistency in tidewater fishing," says legendary BASS pro Roland Martin. "When you figure a tide pattern, you can plan your fishing easily. But you've got to move fast, and 'run the tide.'

"Whatever pattern you find that works, you can basically run ahead of the tide, duplicating any pattern for a period of time by staying ahead of it. The tide doesn't arrive at, say, 10 o'clock throughout the whole tidal river. It's not all high at the same time. Say you have a 100-mile tidal system, it's going to take many hours for the tide to get to the upper end."

Although tidewaters are not as often touted for

their bass productivity as are reservoirs, brackish water rivers and bays are among the most fertile, fish-filled places to find largemouth. Tidal rivers and lakes have a natural ebb and flow of water that acts as a tremendous "flushing" or cleansing agent. Many people, in fact, believe this flushing action is the reason largemouth fishing can be so excellent in tidewaters right in major industrial cities, where one would expect pollution to take a toll.

Another reason tidal zones offer topnotch bass fishing is that the forage base is far more diverse and prolific than many lake environments, which are more contained. In most tidal waters where largemouth bass live, a seasonal influx of saltwater life provides gamefish with food.

For example, American, hickory and Alabama shad migrate up many coastal rivers to spawn. After the shad hatch into fry, they migrate back downstream to the open ocean, where they live until maturity, eventually running back up their natal rivers to spawn.

Such shad fry provide a fabulous and nearly inexhaustible seasonal food supply for largemouth. Herring, mullet, American eels and other marine fish migrate similarly into brackish water, and are relished by bigmouths, too. Saltwater shrimp, and in some areas menhaden, are found far up tidal rivers and bays and also are outstanding forage for bass.

Food preferences of tidewater bass change seasonally and also can force fish to change locations according to the forage available. Naturally, it be-

SHRIMP-IMITATING baits
are productive soft plas-
tics for tidal bass.

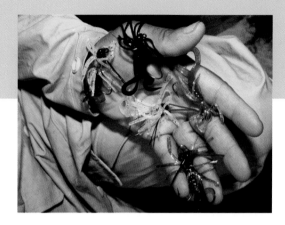

hooves fishermen to know the forage bass prefer at any given time, and where such food is likely to be found in the tidal water targeted.

When giant schools of American shad fry begin migrating to the open ocean, it's a good bet lots of largemouth will be nearby, feeding on them. Shad schools often can be seen in very early mornings as they ripple the surface, usually in broad, open expanses of water. Normally, shad schools move slowly with current, and it's not unusual to see several different shad schools at a time in calm water.

Sometimes bass can be seen at the surface charging into the shad, which makes for outstanding topwater fishing. Small plugs that resemble shad draw strikes.

However, the best fishing more often is found deep, where jigs, crankbaits and especially epoxy streamer flies score very well on bass feasting on migrating shad fry.

High, slack tide can make for tough fishing, because bigmouth scatter to feed. Bass can work into very shallow, brush-filled or marshy water. Long casts with searching lures like crankbaits, weedless spoons and spinnerbaits can be effective.

Most knowledgeable tidewater bass anglers, however, avoid slack tides, especially high ones. Instead they run to areas where the water is moving, and many fishermen prefer falling tides. This situation drains water off flats, which brings baitfish with it. During the latter parts of falling tides, many flats have almost no water, so bass often station on the first dropoff nearby to feed on bait swept their way.

Feeder creek mouths can be especially good during ebb tides. Many such places have sandbars at their mouths, which are excellent bass structures. But don't just work the bars if no bass are caught. Moving deeper, into 10, 12, 15 even 20 feet of water off of a creek mouth, may be necessary to locate schools of big bass feeding on bait swept out with a falling tide.

Shoreline-connected sandbars or, better yet, oyster or mussel shellbars that flood during incoming tides can hold good schools of bigmouth. Shellbars teem with aquatic life that draws tiny minnows, which in turn attracts feeding largemouth, striped bass and catfish. Equally attracted are saltwater fish such as red drum, spotted sea trout, flounder, snook and tarpon. Small islands far from shore that become covered during high tides are similarly productive for bass.

Many tidal rivers and bayous have well-defined ledges, which are premier bass holding structures. Ledges usually are made of mud or hard clay with some shell mixed in, and are the result of many years of tidal current sweeping against the bottom at varying depths, according to tide stage.

Ledges can be productive during any tide stage. A ledge often will be many yards from the bank during flood tides, and it's not unusual for a ledge to be covered by 6 or 8 feet of water when the tide is high. Through experience, tidewater bass anglers learn the locations of ledges, but a sensitive depthfinder, particularly a graph unit, is extremely helpful. The use of bottom bumping plugs also helps find ledges. Crankbaits, jigs and plastic worms are excellent tools for learning where ledges are located.

Unlike "hot" lakes, many of America's tidewaters are uncrowded, unpressured bass havens, full of fish and lacking in anglers.

SMALL CRANKBAITS are tough to beat in tidal fisheries. They can imitate a host of forage the bass usually feed on.

INDEX